A Skeptic's
Guide
to Writers'
Houses

Anne Trubek

UNIVERSITY OF PENNSYLVANIA PRESS

PHILADELPHIA · OXFORD

Illustrations by John Hubbard

Published by
University of Pennsylvania Press
Philadelphia, Pennsylvania 19104-4112
www.upenn.edu/pennpress

Printed in the United States of America on acid-free paper
10 9 8 7 6 5 4 3 2 1

Library of Congress Cataloging-in-Publication Data
Trubek, Anne.
   A skeptic's guide to writers' houses / Anne Trubek.
Includes bibliographical references.
ISBN: 978-0-8122-4292-8 (hardcover : alk. paper)
1. Authors, American—Homes and haunts.   2. Literary
landmarks—United States.   3. Authors and readers—United
States.   4. American literature—appreciation—United States.
PS141.T78   2011
810.9B 22   2010021358

Contents

Emily Dickinson's
chamber pot

Chapter 1

The Irrational Allure of Writers' Houses

AROUND THE TIME the housing collapse hit New York City, a modest one-bedroom apartment came up for sale on the Lower East Side. "How quiet, serene, and wonderful is this 1-bedroom apartment with balcony?" the real estate ad asked. "So quiet, serene and wonderful that one of the top 5 best novels of 2006 . . . was written here!"

The novel was *Absurdistan*, the writer Gary Shteyngart, a rising literary star, who was born in Leningrad in 1972 and then immigrated to New York at the age of seven. Shteyngart's generation-late Russian immigrant sensibility, brilliant word play, and omnipresence on the New York literary scene has made him downtown hipster cool as well as the subject of esoteric academic conference presentations.

His apartment, in Coop Village, sits in a bleak unadorned building that neighbors other similarly grim structures. Perhaps, not unintentionally, Shteyngart's Loho digs resemble the landscapes of the Soviet-era Russia he conjures in his fiction.

The ridiculous real estate ad—come live where *Absurdistan* was written!—and the fittingly utilitarian architecture of the apartment building drew two bloggers from DowntownNY to take a tour. They pretended to be prospective buyers, and furtively shot snaps of Shteyngart's couch and books. They found a photo of a cosmonaut candy bar on one wall, and multiple copies of Shteyngart's novels on his bookshelf.

But no one lay down earnest money. Two months later, in June 2009, the *New York Times* ran a story on local real estate values. Shteyngart's apartment was featured again, having languished on the market, and the price had been reduced by $25,000. The *Times* interviewed agents: was this one-bedroom a good buy? Yes, they answered, based upon dollars per square foot, comparable properties, and the presence of a balcony. The owner's literary celebrity was not a factor.

So much for the presence of a famous writer adding value to a property. Other realtors have tried similar campaigns to no avail. In 2007, the price of Joseph Heller's former East Hampton home was slashed month after month. "It needs a bit of work, and most buyers don't want a project," remarked an agent of why no one wanted the beach home of the author of *Catch-22*. In St. Louis, a house that T. S. Eliot lived in was excitedly touted as a one-of-a-kind historical find for months before it was taken off the market.

You cannot blame agents for thinking a famous writer as former owner might help sell a place. There is a healthy market for peeks inside the homes of authors dead and alive. The *Guardian* runs a weekly series called "Writers' Rooms: Portraits of the Spaces Where Authors Create." (Margaret Drabble has a jigsaw table and works puzzles much of the day.) *Oprah at Home* magazine recently featured "Five Legendary Writers' Homes" (Eudora Welty's secretary, Edith Wharton's view). Coffee-table books are popular holiday gifts: *American Writers at Home* and *Writers' Houses,* for instance, marry sumptuous photographs with short essays about the authors' habits—what they ate for breakfast, where they hung the family photos. The *New York Times* often profiles authors with new releases in features that have photos of writers inside their living rooms or studies, to the delight of readers. Twitter links to such stories are often accompanied by the excitement of seeing Margaret Atwood's garden, or Paul Auster's wood desk.

One could chalk up this fascination with the private lives of authors to celebrity lust—a highbrow version of reading *Us Weekly* to see the latest pictures of Lindsay Lohan's escapades, or a cultured version of reading a profile of a Brooke Astor's son in *Vanity Fair*. There is also a religious strain, a secular form of paying homage. A novelist friend of mine told me that when he went to Stendhal's grave, he kissed it.

Tombstones are popular, but houses are the most popular places in which to engage in literary voyeurism, worship or, more crudely, lit porn. Such has been the case since the fourteenth century, when the town of Arezzo preserved Petrarch's birthplace—where he never lived and about which he cared little. (The current Arezzo house, still open to the public, is a reconstruction. Another Petrarch house, in Arquà, may also be visited, and has been a tourist site since the early nineteenth century.)

Writers' house museums have been on the itineraries of the European Grand Tour since the sixteenth century. By the eighteenth century you could visit Shakespeare's house in Stratford-upon-Avon and leave with a souvenir. Sir Walter Scott anticipated that tourists would one day visit his house, Abbotsford, when he was no longer alive, and indeed they started doing so once it opened shortly after his death in 1832. Haworth, the home of the Brontë sisters, opened around 1928 and continues to draw throngs of tourists on "Brontë land" tours and other excursions. Goethe's birthplace in Frankfurt, Germany, has been a destination spot since 1863, and was carefully reconstructed after it was destroyed in World War II.

In the United States, writers' houses started to be preserved at the end of the nineteenth and the beginning of the twentieth century, when historic preservation and tourism, both ways to shore up and create national memory, rose in cultural value. The first writer's house to open to the public was probably the Henry Wadsworth Longfellow house in 1901.

Things have only picked up since, both here and abroad. Anne Frank's house in the Netherlands may be the most famous and heavily visited writer's house devoted to a twentieth-century writer, and it is a chilling homage indeed. Britain's official tourism guide, VisitBritain.com, projected that 2009 would be a big year for literary tourism; in August Agatha Christie's house in Devon opened as a National Trust property and Alfred Lord Tennyson's Farringford house on the Isle of Wight opened as well.

Today there are about fifty-seven writers with houses in their honor open to the public. Several have more than one house museum, bringing the total number of writers' houses to seventy-three open to the public in the United States. The number is constantly changing: some houses close, others open up. A community development corporation in Cleveland bought Langston Hughes's old home in late 2009 at a sheriff's sale for $17,000 for possible use as a museum. Even fictional places are being restored: a group in Kentucky is rehabilitating a replica of Uncle Tom's Cabin. Norman Mailer's house became a writers' colony a year and a half after his death. Hundreds of thousands of tourists visit these scattered houses—60,000 a year to Mark Twain's Hartford house alone; 20,000 a year to William Faulkner's Rowan Oak in Oxford, Mississippi.

So maybe some enterprising literature lover should snap up that Shteyngart apartment, wait the writer out, and open it up as a museum after his death. Could be a smart literary investment, like buying a signed first edition of *The Da Vinci Code*. There are risks, though. You never know how prices will go on the Lower East Side. And you might make the wrong literary bet.

The last few years have taught us all the fundamental irrationality of real estate. All our houses sit on shaky foundations, terra firma a mirage of trumped-up securities. A mansion in Orange County, California, goes from being the object of a bidding war, jacking the price up a few more million in 2007, to a $50,000 cash-for-keys deal in 2008. So too is literary celebrity subject to the whims of the aesthetic market. Twenty-some years ago, literary critics said the same thing about literature that we are now saying about real estate. There is no bedrock certainty, the academics announced. A classic can become pulp just as a penthouse can become a foreclosure. Hamlin Garland was a big literary deal in his day, a midwesterner who moved to New York and shook up the establishment. Someone bought his house in Wisconsin and made it into a museum. Today, Garland is mostly known as a stumper in the *New York Times Sunday Magazine* crossword. Not many show up to tour his house. There are no sure bets.

Why do we preserve these houses authors live in? Why do we visit them?

If you are trying to preserve literary history, you could do a dozen more sensible things than convert an old (and ever growing older) house into a museum. First of all, houses are not the product of writers. Books are. But

I suppose it would be impractical to build, say, a big book for people to wander inside. You can build a literary theme park: British authors have the market cornered here with Dickens World in Kent. And then there's the Wizarding World of Harry Potter that opened in Orlando in 2010. But a house? It is not an ideal site for a museum. Authors' houses are often tucked away in residential areas, are often quite small, and require endless maintenance, as all homeowners know.

There are many forms of literary worship other than homes, of course. One could visit graveyards, or places where works of literature are set, or collect signatures of the author. Houses, however, take on a particularity unique to their function. They are both private and public: We fight in our pajamas with our spouses, but we also clean up and entertain guests.

Artists get art museums as a vacation destination for lovers of paintings, and composers get the symphony hall. Writers produce art that is easily reproducible and accessible, but offer no common meeting spot, gathering place, or shrine-ready structure. They have, though, usually slept inside a home, and so we make of these homes de facto shrines.

Writers' house museums expose the heartbreaking gap between writers and readers. Part of the pull of a writer's house is the desire to get as close as possible to the precise, generative, "Aha!" But we can never get there. The houses become theaters of Zeno's paradox: writer and readers are already severed from the act of writing. Writers' houses are like writing: at once themselves (marks on paper; a desk) and something else (emotions; a site of literary creativity). They are teases: they ignite and continually frustrate our desire to fuse the material with the immaterial, the writer with the reader.

For me, writers' houses are by definition melancholy. They are often obscure, undervisited, quiet, and dark. They remind me of death. And they aim to do the impossible: to make physical—to make real—acts of literary imagination. Going to a writer's house is a fool's errand. We will never find our favorite characters or admired techniques within these houses; we can't join Huck on the raft or experience Faulkner's stream of consciousness. We can only walk through empty rooms full of pitchers and paintings and stoves.

The curators at writers' house museums rarely seem to get this. They are often astoundingly sincere, prompting in me a knee-jerk cynicism. This is the site of creative genius, they tell us with a straight face, as we stand in kitchens filled with period-appropriate cups and saucers, laid out as if the great man himself had just stepped out for a walk, while a German couple takes pictures of the table with their cell phones.

You cannot line up a list of the greatest American writers with a list of writers' houses open to the public. The canon does not correlate with museums. Just because you are or have been one of the most famous writers in America does not score you a house museum. Of course, there is little consensus as to who are the greatest American writers. Academics disagree. Does Jack London count? How about Ayn Rand? Plus, the general public's conception of the "greats" is often at odds with academic trends. John Steinbeck is often one of the first names Americans will cite when thinking of our "best," and he is almost universally taught in schools. But few academics study him these days—though, of course, his reputation may spike back up again someday. The canon is malleable, subject to trends.

Modern Library's list of the hundred greatest English-language novels lists many American authors with no house museums: Theodore Dreiser (works ranking 16th, 33rd), Carson McCullers (17th), Kurt Vonnegut (18th), Ralph Ellison (19th), Richard Wright (20th), Saul Bellow (21st, 81st), John Dos Passos (23rd), Sherwood Anderson (24th), Henry James (26th, 27th, 32nd), Robert Penn Warren (36th), Thornton Wilder (37th), James Baldwin (39th), James Dickey (42nd), Henry Miller (50th), Philip Roth (52nd), Dashiell Hammett (56th), Walker Percy (60th), John Cheever (63rd), J. D. Salinger (64th), Sinclair Lewis (68th), Nathanael West (73rd), Wallace Stegner (82nd), E. L. Doctorow (86th), Erskine Caldwell (91st), William Kennedy (92nd), William Styron (96th), James M. Cain (98th), Booth Tarkington (100th).

The "greats" on the list *with* houses are much fewer: William Faulkner (6th, 35th, 54th), John Steinbeck (10th), Edith Wharton (58th, 69th), Willa Cather (61st), and Jack London (88th). The top American work in the list, at number two, is F. Scott Fitzgerald's *The Great Gatsby* (James Joyce's *Ulysses* sits at the top). *The Great Gatsby* is a double winner—an American great that is both a popular and a scholarly hit, taught in high schools and beloved by the arbiters of taste. The only preserved Fitzgerald house is in Montgomery, Alabama, where he and Zelda lived for a few months.

It is illogic everywhere: who gets a house, which ones are most beloved. One can make no more sense of why some houses attract more visitors than others, or even why people decide to visit them. I have tried and failed to crunch the numbers into any discernible pattern. According to curator and tour-guide estimates, about half of the visitors to the Whitman house in Camden, New Jersey, come because of their interest in the author. (The rest are interested in American history, and visit after going to see a nearby World War II battleship.) Ten percent of the visitors to the Thomas Wolfe Memorial come specifically for the author. (The majority, however, simply like to visit historic houses.) Half of the visitors to Hemingway's house in Key West are there to celebrate the great writer. (The other half comes to see all the cats that live there.)

Poets do not draw more visitors than novelists. Women writers host no more visitors than men. Nineteenth- and twentieth-century writers are roughly equal. The location of the house and the wealth of the author contribute slightly. Most people who visit the lavish Mount in tourist-friendly Lenox, Massachusetts, do so because they have tickets to Tangle-wood that night and they have some time to kill; only about one tenth of the people who visit the Mount make it to the nearby Melville house. It's in depressed, industrial Pittsfield, and it's a small, rather ordinary dwelling.

Fourteen of the seventy-three sites I've tallied are homes to women writers; five of those are of women writers who had children. Three are dedicated to African American writers. Seventeen poets have houses in their honor, compared to twenty-nine novelists and one playwright. Nonfiction writers total ten. Nineteen writers died in the nineteenth century; forty in the twentieth. The Northeast has the most houses, followed by the South, the Midwest, and the West. Some authors have more than one house open to the public: Edgar Allan Poe and Ernest Hemingway have three each; and John Greenleaf Whittier, among others, has two.

Despite the fact that the first image one has of a house usually involves a family, and the sentimental core of family is a mother and child, there are few houses you can visit where a woman writer lived with her children—the most famous, probably, is the residence maintained in honor of Harriet Beecher Stowe. Her home in Hartford, right next door to the Mark Twain house, receives only one-fifth of the visitors that the latter receives.

To be considered a writer's house, typically the residence must have been home to the author at some point in their life, though when they accomplished or what transpired under the roof varies. For instance, several museums are childhood homes that, in a fictionalized form, figure in the author's works: The Willa Cather Childhood Home in Red Cloud, Nebraska, for example, appears in *My Ántonia*, as the Thomas Wolfe Memorial in Asheville, North Carolina, is a setting in *Look Homeward, Angel*. Others are sites in which their former inhabitants penned great works: Eugene O'Neill wrote *Long Day's Journey Into Night* at Tao House in Danville, California; Edgar Allan Poe National Historic Site in Philadelphia, Pennsylvania, saw the birth of "The Fall of the House of Usher." Others are simply birthplaces—Walt Whitman's Birthplace in West Hills, New York, and Nathaniel Hawthorne's birthplace in Salem, Massachusetts, for example, from which one could only squeeze the most tenuous nurture argument.

As a group, writers' house museums have no umbrella organization. They do not have their own Library of Congress subject terms ("literary landmarks" is as close as it gets). They are an ill-fitting subset of several larger categories: museum, historic houses, and literary history. They are maintained by a dizzying array of institutions. Five are operated by the National Park Service including the Carl Sandburg House in Flat Rock, North Carolina; the Henry Wadsworth Longfellow National Historic Site in Cambridge, Massachusetts; O'Neill's Tao House; Wayside, home of five authors, including Nathaniel Hawthorne and Louisa May Alcott, in Concord, Massachusetts; and the Edgar Allen Poe House in Philadelphia. They are some of the best run and most carefully curated in the country. State historic societies run twelve sites. Counties run many more of these houses, and numerous others are maintained by private foundations. One, Hemingway's Key West house, is a for-profit business venture.

If there's one thing the past hundred years or so seems to tell us, it is that houses are venerated places, sources of nostalgia and sentiment; one thing the past few years or so have taught us is that they are also expensive to own. The old houses of dead authors are only getting older—and they are becoming increasingly costly to maintain. The ceiling of Emily Dickinson's house in Amherst, Massachusetts fell in recently. Staffs across the country are continually wrestling with ways to bring in cash to repaint, renovate, reroof. Many of these sites were founded in hopes that the sites would draw tourists and help local economies. Very few of them, however, bring in enough visitors to see any appreciable uptick in revenue. More often than not, the houses are beset by financial problems, though they receive less press than did the recent crises at the Twain and Wharton houses.

During the 2008 housing free fall, both the Mark Twain house in Hartford, Connecticut, and Edith Wharton's The Mount in Lenox, Massachusetts, faced foreclosure. News of these houses' troubles spread throughout the literary world. Living famous authors, literati, and cultured folks rallied around both houses, decrying the financial pinch, imploring us to send donations to keep these institutions going. A public relations blitz spread across web sites read by bookish types. One would seem churlish— philistine even—not to care about the future of the Mark Twain House.

Yet during these same weeks, The Kate Chopin House in Cloutierville, Louisiana, burned to the ground, oddly echoing Brock Clarke's 2007 novel about writers' houses *An Arsonist's Guide to Writers' Houses in New England*. The Chopin house will not be rebuilt: the cost is prohibitive. The future of that house was over, not just uncertain, like the Twain and Wharton houses. But the devastating fire attracted no notice, no headlines, no funding drives, no stump speeches to our literary heritage. A few months later, Langston Hughes's former house in Cleveland, Ohio was foreclosed on. A small news item in the *Cleveland Plain Dealer* noted its passing, but only those few left who still read the local daily knew about his house's demise.

Before the T. S. Eliot house went on the market, its realtors contacted the T. S. Eliot Society to see if they might want to buy the house. But the asking price, $775,000, was way beyond the means of this small group of scholars and fans. Others have taken the residency route. The Jack Kerouac Project in Orlando, Florida, offers long-term residencies in the house Jack and his mother lived in when he wrote *On the Road*. The James Merrill Writer-in-Residence Program, which also offers stipends and use of the poet's house, and the Amy Clampitt Residency Program offers something similar in the Berkshires. If you are researching Twain, you can spend two weeks in his Quarry Farm house in Elmira, New York.

Raising objections to writers' house museums is like taking on a sacred cow. Restored writers' houses, open to the public, are hard to argue against; like reading, they seem to be obvious societal goods and cultural pieties. But arguments against preserving houses have been made. An early detractor was the writer Charlotte Perkins Gilman, who objected to the construction of these sites along feminist lines: "The home was an ancient and repressive institution, ill suited to the needs of modern social progress in general and women specifically," she wrote in 1903, challenging the "unquestioning acceptance of the home as something perfect, holy, quite above discussion." Gilman linked home to history and memory, asserting that, "the main basis of this homes-sanctity idea is simply the historic record of our ancient religion of ancestor-worship." She called such worship an atavistic "race habit."

Gilman objects to the rampant nostalgia that often underlies these houses. Nostalgia, a desire for an idealized past, is a form of homesickness. To put it cynically, one might say house museums are plagued by illness, as they are established as a retreat to honor a better, other time that never existed. Houses that also serve as a locus of national nostalgia—as do Mark Twain's houses in Hartford, Connecticut, and Hannibal, Missouri—risk becoming conservative loci of an imaginary better, sweeter America, papering over unpleasantries and historical truth.

I have been able to deduce that the American writers with the most devoted fans are Ernest Hemingway and Emily Dickinson—strange bedfellows indeed. Emily Dickinson's Homestead might just be the number-one literary pilgrimage site in the United States. The curator showed me a drawer filled with anonymous gifts and offerings that have been left in the house over the years and discovered by volunteers at closing time, including a silhouette that was found rolled up and hidden behind the radiator in the back parlor. Some people send the poet mail. On her birthday, the mailman delivers envelopes addressed to Emily Dickinson. One year, a greeting card arrived at the house, although it was addressed to Emily Dickinson's gravesite. Inside the card, bearing the words "A Belated Birthday Wish," was a handwritten poem:

> My well-wishes are a century and- ten too late;
> I look forward to the day
> When I may—in person—lay
> A bouquet upon your grave.

I find these homages fascinating but incomprehensible. Who goes to the drugstore and scans the selection of Hallmark cards, trying to decide which would be best to send to a graveyard?

F. Scott Fitzgerald nails this temptation to parody these sites, despite great social and cultural pressure to adore them. One of Fitzgerald's houses—in St. Paul, in which he wrote much of *This Side of Paradise*—is a National Historic Landmark, given its association with Fitzgerald, but not a museum. In 2004, a group of local Fitzgerald fans lobbied to have his birthplace on 481 Laurel Avenue also declared a National Literary Landmark. A professor at the University of Minnesota, Richard McDermott, had lived there for thirty years, and invited many Fitzgerald fans in for a visit. Its new National Landmark designation came with a plaque, but the house is still not a museum.

Probably a good thing, too. In 1924, when Fitzgerald was famous, the British magazine *Country Life* wrote a feature, "Ten Houses for Ten Authors." They imagined what American writers' houses should be like. It is a fanciful piece—based upon the authors' fiction, what should their houses look like? Zane Grey, they wrote "would be perfectly happy, we feel, in a 'dobe ranch house set in the midst of the sunburnt mesa. But like his stories, it should be colorful." The tad-too-literal piece imagines Fitzgerald's house as a castle. It has stairways that go nowhere ("like Scott Fitzgerald's stories") and rococo pillars decorated with "cocktail glasses, maraschino cherries, bottles, and dollar signs."

In 1936, Fitzgerald wrote a story called "An Author's House." He begins by noting that he reads many accounts of Hollywood celebrities at home, "usually with the hostess done up from behind with a bib explaining how on God's earth to make a Hollywood soufflé," but then goes on to write that it had been some time since he had read one of an author's house. So he instead chose to give an imaginary tour of his own fancifully literary home to a reporter. He begins in the basement. "It's everything I've forgotten," says the author. "All the complicated dark mixture of my youth and infancy that made me a fiction writer instead of a fireman or a soldier."

He goes to the bedroom where, "I write a good deal lying down and when there are too many children around, but in summer it's hot up here in the daytime and my hand sticks to the paper." When the visitor moves some cloth onto a chair the author yells: "Don't touch that! It's just the way somebody left it."

They go to the attic, which "was the attic of Victorian fiction. It was pleasant, with beams of late light slanting on piles and piles of magazines and pamphlets and children's school books and college year books and 'little' magazines from Paris and ballet programs and the old Dial and Mercury and L'Illustration unbound and the Nicholas and the journal of the Maryland Historical Society, and piles of maps and guide books from the Golden Gate to Bou Saada. There were files bulging with letters, one marked 'letters from my grandfather to my grandmother' and several dozen scrap books and clipping books and photograph books and albums and 'baby books' and great envelopes full of unfiled items."

"This is the loot," the author says grimly. "This is what one has instead of a bank balance."

When the tour ends, the "visitor said, half apologetically: 'It's really just like all houses, isn't it?'"

The author nodded. "I didn't think it was when I built it, but in the end I suppose it's just like other houses after all."

I often find the experiences of visiting these houses deadening, so I kept asking others why they seek them out. Friends and family and curators and visitors continually tell me how moving they find these houses. They'd tell me a story about how they were transfixed by the sight of Jack London's typewriter behind glass in a diorama of his study. A curator at Melville's Arrowhead tells me she regularly sees "crusty old men" tear up when they stand in the doorway of the writer's second-floor study overlooking Mount Greylock, the double-humped mountain that inspired a white whale.

My friend Ellen, a historian, offers me her reasons: "We know the thing isn't really there, but we want a touchstone to imagine with, we want to know that others also come here to imagine the same thing, we want some sort of material connection with the thing that is gone and irrecoverable."

But that's the rub: it is gone and irrevocable.

Clearly, though, I am protesting too much. After all, I keep going. It is too easy to adopt an underlying attitude of derision, the observer pointing out errors and oddities, the whole faux simulated nature of it all. The truth is, I am addicted to these stories of spiritual fulfillment, the hushed performances of empathy, and the acts of supplication to the aura of creative genius I have found at the twenty or so writers' houses I have visited. I may not cry when I stand in Melville's study, but I do when I stand behind those old men tearing up in his study, or holding the cards people send to "Emily."

This emotion, earned only at the cost of being once removed, makes me as sad as do the houses, melancholy monuments to death. There is something curious and ultimately insatiable about visiting a dead writer's house. It has something to do with pilgrimage, the hushed aura of sacredness; it has something to do with history; one life preserved. It has something to do with loss, and objects as compensation for loss. And it has something to do with the way literature works, with the longing created by the fact that words separate writers from readers yet create an ineluctable intimacy between the two, structured by marks on paper.

This book is an account of my vexed journey across America visiting writers' houses, a long trip taken in order to figure out their allure. I first conceived of it long ago as a reverse travel guide, a guide to places you shouldn't bother to visit, to misdirected spiritual quests and middlebrow, wrongheaded approaches to reading and writing. It is not coincidental that I came up with this idea of skewering writers' houses while a graduate student in English, studying American literature under the tutelage of post-modernism. Just as we can read a literary work any way we chose, regardless of authorial intention, I decided we could go to house museums with any attitude we desire, reverent or snide. My premise was that we need not honor them, or consider them holy and unassailable. We can read them, as I do in this book, against the grain.

And yet while I found some houses so sincere they seem lifted from Fitzgerald's "An Author's House," at each house I also fell a little bit in love, if not with the airbrushed stories some museums tell. Looking in the corners for dust bunnies or down the block at the neighborhood or deep in the biographies or letters of the authors, I found stories that told me something authentic about literature, politics, history, and contemporary America.

At the Walt Whitman House in Camden I rediscovered Whitman's poetry, as well as the history of Camden. At Mark Twain's houses in Hannibal and Hartford I thought about the boundaries between fact and fiction, a topic that Twain—or I should say Samuel Clemens—thought about brilliantly, and that Hannibal regrettably thinks about too little. In Concord, Massachusetts, the American mecca of writers' houses, I thought about the history of historic preservation, and discovered that of all the eminences who had lived there, the most unlikely one—Louisa May Alcott—best exemplifies the myth of the Romantic artist. Ernest Hemingway, who has four preserved houses in his honor, led me to Key West, Florida, Ketchum, Idaho and, vicariously, to Cuba, where the always ideological nature of writers' houses is on display, as they are currently embroiled in very contemporary political debates. At Thomas Wolfe's house in Asheville, North Carolina, I contemplated the vagaries of the literary canon, as well as the important work that curators at writers' houses perform. The burnt remains of Jack London's dream house caused me to wonder about the impossibility of predicting one's posthumous life. In Dayton, Ohio, I shed tears for Paul Laurence Dunbar, his mother, and his long-time readers, as well as for the rust belt today. Edgar Allan Poe's houses in Philadelphia, Baltimore, and the Bronx are sadly unchanged monuments to American urban poverty and decay, during Poe's lifetime and today. Finally, at home in Cleveland I wondered what we lose when we fail to restore a writer's house.

This is an idiosyncratic guide to be sure: it will not help you plan literary travel, and the chapters do not represent a diverse cross-section of authors, regions, or time periods. This means excluding many houses I have visited as well as those I have yet to tour.

I chose to tell stories that revealed to me something beyond biography or author-worship, be it about the literary canon and its discontents, the futility of planning one's posthumous life, or economic development in postindustrial cities. I have found these narratives among the childhood anecdotes and descriptions of furniture—the attic of Victorian fiction, as Fitzgerald put it. Infusing each chapter is the question of how we imagine the writers behind the pages we read, the necessary but vexed relationship between author and reader.

You and I we are not exempt from this last concern. After you have finished my tour of writers' houses, or even if you wander off midway through, we will have formed a relationship. You can make it, and me, into anything you desire.

Mickle Boulevard, Camden

Chapter 2

Trying to Find Whitman in Camden

THE FIRST WRITER'S HOUSE I visited was the Walt Whitman house in Camden, New Jersey. It was 1991, the economy was in the tank, and I had just fled to a Ph.D. program in English.

In the early 1990s, poststructuralist theory was de rigueur in graduate studies of literature, and I had signed on. I approached English as a way to play with meaning, language, and form, and not as a way to understand what the great authors I read initially intended. The scribe was dead; we were dancing upon his grave. In "The Death of the Author," a touchstone text for the theory revolution of the 1980s (although first published in 1967), the words of French literary critic Roland Barthes set the stage: "We know that to give writing its future, it is necessary to overthrow the myth: the birth of the reader must be at the cost of the death of the Author."

A liberating idea for a literary critic, to be sure. The reader is the locus of meaning, and may do with the words as she wills; the biography of an author, or her intentions for that matter, don't mean squat. Those who believe otherwise, those who worship at the shrine of the "great man," who are fascinated by trivialities like Shakespeare's mistress, Shelley's early death, or Hemingway's drinking, have it all wrong. They are unsophisticated readers mired in a middlebrow concept of individuality and celebrity gossip, a realm of literature loving that Barthes calls "ordinary culture," where "the image of literature to be found in ordinary culture is tyrannically centered on the author, her person, his life, his tastes, his passion."

When I found the brochure to the Walt Whitman house, it seemed to perfectly describe to me what was wrong with ordinary culture: "The Walt Whitman House provides an intimate glimpse into the . . . poet's life . . . through . . . original letters, personal belongings, the bed in which he died, and the death notice that was nailed to the front door."

I decided to go to Camden to expose not simply Whitman's house, but all of the writers' house museums as the frauds I believed them to be. I would skewer them, branding them as Piranesi drawings of literary impossibility. Is the author under there? Nope! Is he up those stairs? Gotcha again! Visiting this house would not equal, enhance, or illuminate Whitman's masterful "Song of Myself." Places like these, I was sure, were intended for people who like to think of themselves as cultured readers but are not. The writers' house museums, I decided, were middlebrow.

It was a typical mid-Atlantic November day—thirty-four degrees, gray, with a wet wind—when I drove over the Benjamin Franklin Bridge from Philadelphia to Camden. As I arrived, it was "garbage storming," a particular weather pattern indigenous to northeastern urbanity, where trash is borne aloft by winter breezes. Camden is a scarier, darker doppelganger of Philadelphia, thick with the promise of aggression.

"The Walt Whitman House is easy to miss," its curator told me when I called for directions. "It's a row house like any other, except it's made of wood. It's on Mickle Boulevard, across the street from the county jail. Look for the jail, and you'll find the house." I did indeed locate the house via the jail or, more precisely, people on the sidewalk looking up at the prison. They stood silent, a hand on a hip thrust to the left, a finger circling the air. I followed their gaze up to the building. Squinting, I could see inmates behind the windows gesturing back to the people down below: three fingers pressed against the pane, then a thumb, then an entire hand. The prisoners and their families had invented a language of their own. Later, I did some research on this odd tableau, and found an article in the local paper. "They just try to communicate the best way they know how," said Florence O'Neill, a friend of an inmate. "My daughter knows how to spell 'I love you,'" said prisoner Martin Rodriguez. One year later the city of Camden would sandblast the windows to prohibit prisoners from viewing the street. That bit of life—and language—is gone.

The Walt Whitman House, where another language was invented, remains. Mickle Boulevard is easy to find, but hard to be on. The thoroughfare, close to the water, right off the bridge, is broad—four lanes with a wide median in the middle—made even broader by the lack of traffic. It has an atmosphere of emptiness and menace. Driving down the street, I felt at once insignificant and exposed. The brown concrete expanse of the road and the looming jail made it hard to notice details, or to see anything in particular.

Five small row houses remained intact. These fossils contain the imprints of their torn-down brethren. As their name implies, row houses are packed one next to the other, so when one vanishes, its trace remains. You can see the plaster outlined reminders of what had been stairs and doorways on the sides of the still-standing homes.

The wood-framed Whitman house sits in the middle of this island. The city left a strip of cobblestones in the curb outside the home, so my car started bumping and shaking as I shifted into park. Then I saw the faded, red-painted shingle bearing the words: "Walt Whitman House."

Walt Whitman died in this house. He went to Camden in 1873 to be with his sick mother, who was under the care of Whitman's older brother George. She died one month after Walt arrived. Whitman decided to stay with George and devote himself to writing full-time. He was sixty-five, paralyzed in one leg, in poor health, depressed over his mother's death, and tired of his clerk's job in Washington, D.C. While in Camden, Whitman wrote prolifically, publishing three editions of *Leaves of Grass* as well as his autobiography, *Specimen Days*.

Nine years later, George moved away and urged his older brother to come along. Whitman didn't join him, choosing instead to remain in Camden; though he was chronically poor, he had recently earned modest royalties that in 1884 allowed him to purchase the house on Mickle Street for

$1,750. "Camden was originally an accident, but I shall never be sorry I was left over in Camden," Whitman wrote. "It has brought me blessed returns."

The house is not a Victorian manse or a colonial mansion. Most historic residences are preserved because they are interesting architecturally or just really big—the former haunts of wealthy folks. This house has nothing unusual about it—making it, perversely, unique. "If this weren't Walt Whitman's house, it wouldn't be here," the former curator Margaret O'Neill told me. The house offers visitors a tour of a rarely preserved period style: small, dank rooms brightened by whimsical, often clashing wallpaper and rugs. "This is how most people lived: in small spaces with lots of patterns and different colors all juxtaposed in a tight space," O'Neill says.

The house is set up, as are most house museums, to fool us into thinking that Whitman was still living there. The curators lay cups and saucers and spoons for two on the small kitchen table, and half-finished needlework by the sewing machine. They are trying to compress Whitman's life into a snapshot of a typical day. Time stands still: shoes next to the bed, a book open on a desk.

Since so few visit the house—which holds twenty people—there's no need to rope off the rooms or frame the views. Patrons just wander about. There isn't much to look at, since Whitman never owned much and the house is architecturally ordinary, aside from an enormous number of photographs. Some are hanging on the walls; others are propped up on the floor. Most, however, are left turned down to prevent light damage. Many are reproductions of photographs taken during Whitman's lifetime; the curators flip them up while giving tours. These tiny, faded images provide the evidence for historic reconstructions: the living room photograph shows in which corner Whitman kept his rocking chair. Today, that same rocking chair sits in that very corner.

Most of the images, however, are of the good gray poet himself. Whitman was one of the most photographed men of his time. After all, his formative years were also those of photography. He appears in profile, standing in a field and smiling, in a Christlike pose. There are daguerreotypes, tintypes, and a painting done on oak by a friend (the latter is like the precursor of velvet Elvis paintings). In the dark back parlor, there's a photograph of the viewing of Whitman's body in 1892. A friend who accompanied me jumped when he saw the picture; he had been standing on the very spot where the coffin stood.

The democratic sensibility of photography dovetailed beautifully with Whitman's own literary vision, as he expressed in the preface to *Leaves of Grass*: "In these Leaves everything is literally photographed." Whitman's expansive cataloguing of America and Americans presaged documentary photography, born at the end of Whitman's life, on the cusp of the twentieth century. Whitman believed that compiling portraits of great men could produce a history of the nation. He claimed to have given Mathew Brady the idea for his book of daguerreotypes, *The Gallery of Illustrious Americans* (1850). For Whitman, photographs are poems, and poems are nations: "The United States themselves are essentially the greatest poem." "Rather than having a lot of contradictory records by witnesses or historians—say of Caesar, Socrates, Epictetus, others," he suggested to a friend, "We could have three or four or half a dozen portraits—very accurate—of the men: that would be history—the best history—a history from which there could be no appeal."

Lacking that one incontrovertible photograph of the poet—and his overexcited, belief in image as evidence—the Walt Whitman House strives to find objects that make the best history. All of them are worthy of appeal.

We come to Whitman through words, and these are what remain of him, and these are what change as Mickle Street does. But ironically, his poetry is, as O'Neill put it, the sole reason his house museum exists. Whitman understood our future misplaced desire, and warned us not to go to Camden to find him. "If you want me again look for me under your boot-soles," he advised. But, it seems, we want to find *his* boot-soles. We want to see his stuff.

For reasons like this, museums like this make my brain hurt. They are stuffed with paradoxes. Literary works create imaginary places and aesthetic experiences; authors' homes are furnished with mundane material objects. I will never find Whitman or my favorite characters within these houses; I can't hear the poet singing. I want to get as close as possible to the moment of creation, to that time when pen dipped into ink and out came a line of poetry, I will not find it inside this drafty house in Camden.

Plus, not only are the writers always dead, but writers are always already dead. Socrates figured this out way back when, and feared the spread of writing. It has "no parent to protect [it]," he lamented. "If you ask it a question, it preserve[s] a solemn silence."

Readers desire an impossible intimacy, a desire at once central to the pleasure of reading but ultimately insatiable. We want to get as close as possible to the ideas a writer created and then to roll back even further, to the writer him- or herself. But we never can, just as we can never stop time. The act of reading is always severed from the act of writing. (To test out this hypothesis, try to write about the act of writing at the moment you are writing. Impossible.)

Authors' houses are like writing in this way. Both are material and immaterial. In this, they are like dollar bills: things in themselves and representations of other things. We go to writers' houses to fill in that gap produced by writing only to be presented once again with the impossibility of marrying writer and writing. What we get is a pageant of writing's magical ability to be at once itself and something else.

At the Whitman house, a lot of the past was also wrong. In the poet's second-floor bedroom-cum-study were random pieces of paper strewn across the floor, the curator's attempt to re-create Whitman's sloppy writing habits. But the papers didn't look right. The curator told me he picked them up at Ben Franklin's museum. They have a press there, and they make reproductions of *Poor Richard's Almanac*. But Franklin predates Whitman by a century. I asked the curator some more questions. He bought the quill pen from a stationery shop. He put the compositor stick, a device letterpress printers used to set type, on the mantel of the bedroom because he thought it was cool.

It does not bother me that the curator failed to get Whitman's writing materials right, because even if he had tried harder he would have failed. It literalizes the problem inherent in writers' houses. It is as if the closer we get to the value of a house's existence—that the former denizen wrote there—a centrifugal force sets in, and the objects spin out of historical control.

Whitman, always one step ahead, was obsessed by this insatiable desire to merge things and spirit, readers and writers, too. "The most profound theme that can occupy the mind of man," he writes in his autobiography, "is doubtless involved in the query: What is the fusing explanation and tie—what the relation between the (radical, democratic) Me, the human identity of understanding, emotions, spirit, on the one side, of and with the (conservative) Not Me, the whole of the material objective universe and laws . . . on the other side?"

Whitman longed to overcome the gap of representation, the deadness of the written word, by infusing it with spirit, to have his poems *be* him and not just represent his thoughts:

Camerado! This is no book;
Who touches this touches a man,
(Is it night? Are we here together alone?)
It is I you hold, and who holds you,
I spring from the pages into your arms—decease calls me
forth . . .
I love you, I depart from materials,
I am as one disembodied, triumphant, dead.

You would think visiting the Walt Whitman house might help to fuse and tie Mes to Not-Mes—to be with the poet's things, to stand where he wrote, to capture him as he springs from the pages into our arms. But he has, indeed, departed from materials. Inside the Walt Whitman house on that dismal day, I felt no spirit, no ghosts, and no aura. His boot-soles did nothing for me. I could not conjure up any lines, imagine him composing on the right armrest of his rocking chair, or even speculate on American indifference to its native voices, then or now. I did, however, notice that the house smelled of dust and decay. I heard the blast of the heater. I wondered about rats. The place made me sleepy, like all museums eventually do, and I wished I were home.

At Whitman's seventieth birthday dinner in 1889, a guest predicted that the poet's (eventual) grave in Camden would make the city "known to the world from the fact of one man living and dying here." That has not come to pass. Most Americans are surprised to learn that Whitman ever lived, not to mention died, in Camden. Those who do make the trek to this desolate city, to visit the poet or his restored house, are continually surprised at what they find.

Whitman was already famous by the late nineteenth century when Theodore Wolfe, a journalist working on *Literary Shrines: The Haunts of Some Famous American Authors,* ventured to Camden to interview him for his book. When he arrived at the house, though, Wolfe was disappointed. The trolley conductor dropped him off at 328 Mickle Street. Wolfe thought he had been given the wrong directions. Surely the dingy, small house on the nondescript street could not be that of the genius poet. When he saw the "W. Whitman" plaque on the door, however, he realized he had, indeed, arrived at his destination.

Upon receiving his guest, Whitman suggests they go for a walk. Wolfe notes that everyone on the streets of Camden knows Whitman, though few appear to have read his poetry. The journalist is enchanted by the warm reception the poet receives from passersby. Neighbors go out of their way to say hello. Kids stop their games to run over and greet "Mister Socrates," as they call him. Whitman takes Wolfe to the ferry and to lunch at the hotel—everywhere, everyone smiles and approaches the poet, and he stops and chats with each of them.

Another journalist had a similar experience traveling to interview Whitman. On a muggy August day in 1893, Elbert Hubbard, who had been tracking down writers all over the country for his book *American Authors* (part of a fourteen-volume series called *Little Journeys to the Homes of the Great*), arrived in Camden. Hubbard described the city as a "sandy monotonous waste of straggling buildings." He noticed the row houses and conjectured that speculators must have thought building by the river would turn the place around. "But they reckoned ill, for the town did not boom," he writes, "for the most part the houses of Camden are rented, and rented cheap."

Rain had made mud of the dirt roads. On Mickle Street, "steaming sewage" ran in the gutters and the houses, which were built close to the curb and "seemed to have discharged their occupants into the street." Men stood on stoops smoking, while kids played in the putrid avenue. Trains ran on the road next to Mickle Street, sending soot and smoke "straight over Number 328, where . . . lived the mightiest seer of the century—the man . . . rank[ed] with Socrates, Epictetus, Saint Paul, Michelangelo, and Dante."

Hubbard arrives at the "plain, weather-beaten house," and sees the poet sitting inside. He fumbles for words. Whitman spots the twenty-five-year-old, and, familiar with the cocked-eyebrow surprise of visitors to his house, puts the question to him: "You are wondering why I live in such a place as this?"

"Yes, that is exactly what I was thinking of!" Hubbard replies.

"You think I belong in the country, in some quiet shady place," Whitman begins, and then gives his reasons for his surroundings:

This babble and babel of voices pleases me better, especially since my legs went on a strike, for although I can't walk, you see I still mix with the throng, so I suffer no loss. I like the folks, the plain, ignorant, unpretentious folks; and the youngsters that come and slide on my cellar door do not disturb me a bit. . . . Today an

Irishman passed in three quarts of berries and walked off pretending to be mad because I offered to pay. When he was gone, I beckoned to the babies over the way—they came over and we had a feast.

Despite the romantic sentimentalism Whitman expressed to Hubbard, the poet was known to hate Camden at least as much as he loved it. "It is always painful to come back into the cities—the streets—the stinking reeking streets—Mickle Street—sluttish gutters—women with hair a-flying—dust brooms clouding the streets—confinement—the air shot off. Oh!" he once remarked to his friend Horace Traubel.

While in Camden, Whitman struggled rather comically to shape his own posthumous reception. He issued a "deathbed" edition of *Leaves of Grass*. He sat for hours and hours over days and months telling his final thoughts to Traubel for the nine-volume series *With Walt Whitman in Camden*. Whitman took steps to preserve his physical effects as well. Whereas he paid only $1,750 for his house, he paid $4,000 for an imposing tombstone to be erected in the nearby Harleigh Cemetery. (The carvers initially engraved the dates wrong, so they took off the days of both Whitman's birth and death.) In his will, the poet left his brain to the American Anthropometric Society, to be studied by phrenologists. The brain was delivered, but, shortly thereafter, a lab worker dropped it on the floor.

After his death, all of Whitman's personal effects were removed from the house and divided among the three the executors of his will, a trio that included Traubel. (The home was opened up only on the poet's birthday for members of the Walt Whitman Fellowship, International.) In the early twentieth century, it passed into private hands and became rental housing. In 1919 David Stern, a newspaper publisher, launched a successful local campaign to have the city of Camden buy the residence, after which it was restored and a private group known as the Walt Whitman Foundation hired a curator to oversee it.

In 1940, the foundation received legal status and raised funds to clean up the area around the house, buy more property, and establish a Whitman center. In 1946, one member of the center's board of trustees offered to donate his vast collection to the City of Camden, asking that the city buy the property next to Whitman's to house a fireproof library. The board of trustees tried to "shame Camden into a realization of its unique opportunity to elevate itself," but was unsuccessful, and the collection went elsewhere.

Eventually Whitman's house became the property of the State of New Jersey. They proposed several major initiatives for attracting more visitors to the poet's former residence, which had to be closed in 1990 due to budgetary restrictions. One such scheme called for adding a plaza, library, café, and bookstore to the house. The Camden City Council rejected that idea in 1992. Though Camden has added some successful tourist attractions in the past decade, including the Adventure Aquarium a few blocks away, the Whitman house has only slightly benefited.

Visitors to the Walt Whitman house are no longer struck by the teeming, dirty noise of Mickle Street—instead, "desolate" is a more apt descriptor. In 1979, when Stephanie Kraft visited the residence for her study of writers' houses, *No Castles on Main Street: American Authors and Their Homes*, the view was of "a weed-filled vacant lot stretching to the Campbell Soup plant, which is topped with two towers painted red and white to look like cans of soup." Poet Mark Doty described his unsettling 1996 visit in an ode to the good gray poet:

> We drove to Camden, where your house still stands
> —modest, clapboard, dwarfed by the prison
> glowering across the street, where trucks shock
> themselves percussively on outrageous
> potholes. Jail, detox, welfare: Camden
> accepts it all, Camden's the hole in which
> we throw anything . . .

The jail across the street, like the hustle and bustle on Mickle Street in Whitman's time, is easily wrought into poignant irony. But Margaret O'Neill, echoing Whitman's comments about Camden to Traubel, refuses to sentimentalize a house of human suffering. "It really bothers me when people say, 'Walt would have been right at home with that,'" she says. "What a superficial understanding of Whitman. How can this great champion of freedom have felt comfortable with a prison across the street? And all the wasted lives. I think about how Whitman would have felt and we find evidence in his poetry. Then she quotes from Whitman's "Song of Myself":

> Unscrew the locks from the doors!
> Unscrew the doors themselves from the jambs!

Whoever degrades another degrades me
And whatever is done or said returns at last to me.

I returned to Camden in 2004, this time on a brilliant summer day, blinding light bouncing off newly paved roads. By then I had been tenured as an English professor, and no longer inspired by scholarship, which, anyway, never took hold anywhere but among the small cadre of us who had made it from poststructural theory to an academic sinecure. Ordinary culture still reigns—bloggers take furtive photos of Shteyngart's apartment, and Gawker delights in their trips.

Mickle Street had changed quite a bit. This time it was less like a cliché of abandoned urban poverty and more like a cliché of failed urban renewal: overly broad roads with badly planted medians and not a soul in sight. I took the train, and walked from the busy station to the house, the bustle of commuters suddenly giving way to an empty thoroughfare. It still felt scary, but in a David Lynch way: everything was too bright and too empty.

Sadly, but both predictably and aptly, the sense of the place remained. I want to say the desertedness of Camden sums up despair and hope and promise and futility all at once, since Whitman's day and despite endless retrospective attempts at preservation. But it is too easy to wax lyric about Whitman's obscure and disconcerting death place and bemoan American indifference to its past and always unappreciated poet. It is too easy to render Mickle Street into a literary device: then we would want Camden to remain, as Doty called it, "the hole in which we throw anything."

In his house in Camden, in his deathbed edition of *Leaves of Grass,* Whitman wondered about authors and houses and posterity:

To think of time—of all that retrospection,
To think of to-day, and the ages continued henceforward . . .
To think that the sun rose in the east—that men and
Women were flexible, real, alive—that every thing was alive,
To think that you and I did not see, feel, think, nor bear our part,
To think that we are now here and bear our part . . .
To think the thought of death merged in the thought of
Materials,
To think of all these wonders of city and country, and
Others taking great interest in them, and we taking no
Interest in them.

To think how eager we are in building our houses,
To think others shall be just as eager, and we quite indifferent.

Whitman imagined me imagining him in Camden. I guess this dead author got there before Barthes. He imagined his own death, physical and literary.

Yes, the Walt Whitman house is dead. As dead as Whitman was when he wrote what Barthes would say of all authors: "I am as one disembodied, triumphant, dead."

I did not find Whitman in Camden, but I did find Camden. Inside the house I looked across the street at the jail and the sidewalk below, on which people used to communicate in self-made language.

There was, is, and will be no reason to go to Camden to find Whitman. Even the inmates' friends are gone, along with the language they invented. Whitman knew I would not find him in his old, forgotten house. In fact, he left us all instructions for exactly how to track him down:

If you want me again look for me under your boot-soles.
You will hardly know who I am or what I mean,
But I shall be good health to you nevertheless,
And filter and fibre your blood.
Failing to fetch me at first keep encouraged,
Missing me one place search another,
                    I stop somewhere waiting for you.

Welcome to Hannibal!

Chapter 3

Never the Twain Shall Meet

> Truth is stranger than fiction, but because Fiction is
> obliged to stick to possibilities. Truth isn't.
> —Mark Twain, *Pudd'nhead Wilson's New Calendar* 1897

I WAS LOOKING FORWARD to my trip to Hannibal, which lies 117 miles northwest of St. Louis along the Mississippi River. I visited the town fifteen days before the 2008 presidential election with my nine-year-old son Simon, who still believes in the tooth fairy. A year earlier, I had read him *The Adventures of Tom Sawyer*. He loved it. A rule-follower who idolizes troublemakers, Simon took a shine to Tom. Simon seemed a natural companion for this particular visit, so together we flew to St. Louis, rented a car and headed north on 61, a highway that parallels the Mississippi five miles too far from it to see any water.

As we journeyed north, billboards rose above the fields. "Are We There Yet?" asked one in a childlike script, a question that perversely reminded me of this area's former status as a stop on the Underground Railroad. Plastered below the query was the humongous face of a smiling blond child and a line that read, "Hannibal is only 60 miles away!"

"Getting Closer!" the next billboard said. The ad campaign was working: "We're almost there!" yelled Simon as he leaned his face against the window from his tightly buckled backseat perch.

Eventually we got to a blue water tower with the words "America's Hometown" painted on it. We were in the boyhood home of Samuel Clemens, better known by his penname, the fictional Mark Twain. I had booked us a room at the Hotel Clemens. When we pulled up, Simon was happy to report that in the morning we would be getting a free hot breakfast, according to the red plastic banner strung across the first floor of the low, concrete motel, which sat smack up against the curb of a curving four-lane road. Inside we found the pool just a few steps from the registration desk. It was surrounded by a pale blue four-foot high concrete wall. We peered over it to see painted dolphins and fish cavorting in Day-Glo colors and a green hose limply floating inside a hot tub. The lobby was dark. The door to our room was flimsy, yet hard to open.

Hannibal, Missouri, is the only American town famous solely because of its association with a writer. Other American places associated with authors—Key West, Concord, Oxford—have additional claims to fame. Twain fictionalized the small river town of Hannibal as St. Petersburg in *Tom Sawyer, The Adventures of Huckleberry Finn,* and other lesser-known works. Generations of children have been taught *Huck Finn* in school. It's such a rite of passage that many picture the paradigmatic American boy as a Tom Sawyer with his fishing pole, off to the riverbank.

At age eighty-three, the Argentine writer Jorge Luis Borges agreed to lecture at Washington University in St. Louis only if he was taken to Hannibal. Sick and almost blind, he arrived in Hannibal and put his hand in the Mississippi River. Twain heavily influenced Borges, and the river, in turn, was the source of Twain's inspiration, so Borges wanted to touch it.

While doing preparatory research for my trip, I was taken in by Hannibal's charming, homespun web site announcing Twain-themed exhibits and events. I expected the town to be cute, a fun place to take my kid—hokey in a freshly painted, corny, and midwestern-with-a-southern-drawl-type quaintness. I imagined craft stores filled with model trains, corncob pipes, editions of Twain's novels, and quilts on stands. I expected a Ben Franklin five-and-dime store stocked with necessities and plastic toys. I was hoping for a diner serving homemade biscuits and gravy.

But Hannibal was nothing like I'd expected.

Sam Clemens moved to Hannibal in 1839, when he was four. His father, John Marshall Clemens, built a clapboard house on Hill Street for his family. Clemens was a lawyer and a justice of the peace, but he never made much money at either endeavor. In 1846, too poor to afford the house they had built, the Clemenses moved in with another family in a house across the street, living on its second floor. Clemens's father died in 1847, after which his mother found enough money to move the family back into the house her husband built. Unlike the stereotypical male provider, John Marshall was more of a financial drain than a boon to his family.

When Clemens lived here, slaves were traded near his house. In fact, his father once traded a man named Charley, for $40 worth of tar. When Clemens was ten, he witnessed a master killing a slave with an iron rod in the middle of a Hannibal street: "I knew the man had a right to kill his slave if he wanted to, and yet it seemed a pitiful thing and somehow wrong, though why wrong I was not deep enough to explain," he later recalled. "Nobody in the village approved of that murder, but of course no one said much about it." When another slave was murdered in Hannibal, the author remembered, "Everybody seemed indifferent about it as regarded the slave—though considerable sympathy was felt for the slave's owner, who had been bereft of valuable property by a worthless person who was not able to pay for it."

He lived there until he was seventeen, at which point he left the town permanently and never wanted to return. In his autobiography he remembered Hannibal as "soft, sappy, melancholy."

After Clemens left Hannibal, the rest of his family followed suit. They rented out the Hill Street house, which eventually fell into disrepair. In 1910, when Clemens died, Hannibal was beginning to fade. It had seen the river and railroads bring in more and more money, an influx that had plateaued by 1910, when the lumber industry was also scaling back. In 1911, the old Clemens house was put up for sale, and Hannibal resident and Twain fan George Mahan seized upon it as a potential new source of revenue for the beleaguered town. He bought the house and donated it to the city. Soon thereafter Hannibal started the sorts of tourism efforts that still exist today in the form of the billboards along Highway 61 and the shops and restaurants throughout town and its environs. There is a Huck shopping mall, a Becky Thatcher Restaurant, a Sawyer Creek—there's really no end to the number of establishments Hannibal and its citizens can name after Twain characters. Early on, the town dubbed itself "the Most Famous Small Town in the World" and commissioned statues of Huck and Tom, the first statues erected in America that celebrated fictional characters.

In 1935—the centennial of Clemens's birth—the town dedicated the Mark Twain Museum and held parades and a pageant of "Mark Twain's First One Hundred Years." During the sesquicentennial in 1985, the town swelled with Twain impersonators, Toms, Beckys and people dressed up as Hannibal the Frog. The annual "Tom Sawyer Day"—a festival held each July 4th weekend—started in 1956; and every year since then, Hannibal has crowned a seventh-grade girl and boy "Tom Sawyer" and "Becky Thatcher." Each Tom and Becky busily plays the characters in parades and business openings around town. Beckys are expected to be "as nice and pleasant and friendly" as can be, and wear elaborate costumes made by their mothers with ruffles and bonnets and pantaloons that cost upward of $300. Naturally, in order to become Tom or Becky you must have read *The Adventures of Tom Sawyer*; then you have to take a quiz on Twain and the city of Hannibal and sit for an interview. When the winners are announced, the reigning Tom gives the new Becky a slate, and the reigning Becky gives the new Tom a fishing pole.

I wrote my dissertation on American realism, taking up the thorny questions this mode of literature asks of readers. Can we ever really capture experience through words? Is the pursuit of mimeticism naïve and unsophisticated? Can words ever represent things? I made my case in tortured prose—I was taught to use two verbs when one could do, so I was always "privileging" and "foregrounding" things. But if my prose was suitably *fin de siècle*, my texts were old school, as I analyzed the novels of Theodore Dreiser, Jack London, and Frank Norris—writers read by few these days, though their names may be familiar to many. I claimed that realism, and the aims of realists, are more nuanced than the modernists and postmodernists would have us believe.

My desire to laud the virtues of representing *what is* has always been bound up in my hope that literature can be a powerful force for change by capturing a historic, experiential veracity. If we can show others how things are, change may ensue. To display is to alter.

Although realism is by no means an American invention, it is easy to confuse the aims of realism with another ideological trait, that of the American tendency toward plain style, simplicity, and an anti-intellectual preference for things over ideas, to draw a drive-by summary of how assorted values get clumped together. Tell it like it is. Tell it plain. Be American.

But when it goes too far, realism becomes overly sincere. Sincerity often gets tangled up in American traits such as plain-spokenness, authenticity, and, that most pernicious one, truthfulness. Lionel Trilling argued that sincerity—which he defines as congruence between what one avows and what one feels—is a pre-Enlightenment value, replaced in modernity by authenticity. He may have had a point in light of Shakespeare's thought on the matter, as expressed via Polonius in *Hamlet*: "To thine own self be true!" Sounds obvious, but in a post-Freudian, "who can ever know one's self?" age, it seems naive.

Often, writers' houses try to get as close as possible to the *real*, to historical accuracy. Visitors sometimes arrive with these expectations, too: they want to see how things really were, back then. This desire can lead to some strange preservation gymnastics. At Arrowhead, Herman Melville's home, many come for the view of Mount Greylock. When Melville wrote in this house, he did so in a second-story study. His desk faced the window, out of which he could see Mount Greylock, which he famously said looked like a whale, and inspired Moby Dick. The curve of the tree line made this impression. Today, the trees have grown up, and you have to imaginatively squint to see the mountain as a whale. The curators have considered having the trees cut down so the whale-ish look of the hill will again appear. But this would, of course, entail sacrificing nature for history, swapping one sort of preservation for another.

The best realism realizes its own conceit; it nods to itself, aware of its status as fiction. This is why I love Edith Wharton's The Mount, a few miles away from Arrowhead in Lenox, Massachusetts. In 2002, when The Mount began its centennial celebration, the president and board of the Edith Wharton Restoration, a nonprofit private foundation, decided to commission well-known interior designers, including Bunny Williams and Lady Henrietta Spencer-Churchill, to re-create the rooms "as if the Whartons were living here today." So they put a black laptop on display in the den, a leopard skin rug on the staircase, an abstract expressionist painting in the dining room, and the *Star* and the *Harvard Alumni* magazines on coffee tables.

Of the thousands of comments left by visitors each year, the computer garners the most. But most of the angry comments boil down to this: Why isn't this historically accurate? It's not unusual for visitors to become perplexed when on tour, and the guides patiently explain, over and over, that the furnishings are not meant to evoke the historical period of the Whartons' life. "This is a designer showroom," they are trained to say, "not a historic house."

Many docents, none too enamored of the decorating choices and worn out by visitor reactions, poke fun at the anomalies during tours; my guide pointed out Teddy Wharton's "original 1902 hand-cranked laptop computer" as soon as we stepped into the den. If the guides don't head off questions at the pass, entire tours would devolve into games where guests would guess which objects are authentic and which ones are not.

Whereas many visitors are startled by and angry over the modern interpretation of The Mount, others approach the tour as a sort of shopping trip, asking about china patterns or table dimensions. "We hear a lot of 'Oh honey, I like that color; wouldn't it look nice in our living room?'" one guide told me. The Mount makes it easy for window shoppers to follow up on their finds: business cards advertising china are displayed in the pantry, and, in the catalogue visitors receive with their $16 admission charge, the paint company Benjamin Moore advertises the colors on the walls of the former Wharton residence.

Though many curators desire, and visitors expect to find, a past covered in aspic, it's impossible to turn back time. No amount of money will bring back the large chunk of Edith Wharton's library, that was shipped to England only to be lost in the Blitz, or capture her odd habit of writing in bed every morning and throwing completed manuscript pages to the ground for her maid to collect and collate. While not true to Wharton's experience in almost any manner, The Mount is in some ways the most authentic writer's house in America: By displaying contemporary furnishings, it is authentically itself, an ongoing tribute to a great writer self-consciously adapted in expectation of visitors, rather than a frozen façade of a long-dead author's everyday life.

The Mount doesn't presume to be realistic, so it cannot fail in that aim.

Beyond large infractions, such as the overzealous curator's use of pages from *Poor Richard's Almanac* in the Whitman home, museum workers sometimes introduce more subtle inaccuracies, sneaking in objects the author once owned, even if they don't jive with the history of the house and its inhabitant. For instance, Rowan Oak was not Faulkner's final residence; he moved to Charlottesville, Virginia, two years before his death, leaving the house in Oxford uninhabited. Still, if you visit Rowan Oak today, you will find the house filled with his things—a half-smoked pipe, a pair of muddy boots, several rumpled shirts.

When writers' houses veer over the line into trying to factionalize fiction, as it were, without any awareness they are so doing, they become overly sincere. They take the concept of historic preservation too literally and too far, and end up preserving fiction alongside fact, losing sight of their own institutional role as creators of a fiction, too: the myth of the artist whose reputation they are maintaining. This is also a form of realism gone too far. But this was never a tendency in Twain—quite the opposite.

Part of Twain's genius is that he never lost sight of his own role as fiction-maker (including his name), and reveled in the opportunities the imaginary gave him to enhance the world of fact, to make it more real than a strictly faithful re-creation could ever be. Plus, he took great delight in exploring the sometimes slippery edges between truth and falsehood, sincerity and masquerade. What else are all those twins, those *Pudd'nhead Wilson* and *Prince and the Pauper* and kings and dukes discussing Shakespeare about? Twain, small-town Missouri boy who left the Midwest while young to live an incredibly cosmopolitan life based on the East Coast, always makes fun with breathtaking empathy. Twain knew how to use the conventions of realism and the proclivities of Americans to show us ourselves, leaving us bemused. Twain is considered an iconic American author not because he embodies us—tell it plain, tell it simple—but because he was always *commenting upon* us. "All of American literature comes from *Huckleberry Finn*," Hemingway said; Faulkner called him "The father of American literature." While some Great American Novels traffic in sentiment—one might think of Harriet Beecher Stowe's *Uncle Tom's Cabin* here—Mark Twain was always the first to pillory the American tendency to be gullible, naïve, and lacking in irony. He was utterly insincere.

Yet, in Hannibal, Missouri, the shepherds of Mark Twain's legacy have created a wonderland that is remarkably un-Twainian. Not only do they fall prey to the misinterpretation of sincerity, they appear to have forgotten entirely that Twain's work, like his name, is fictional. Outside the Mark Twain Boyhood Home and Museum is a white fence. In front is one of those historical markers, white with black raised letters and curlicues on top. Only, it is not historical at all. It reads:

> TOM SAWYER'S FENCE
> HERE STOOD THE BOARD
> FENCE WHICH TOM SAWYER
> PERSUADED HIS GANG TO
> PAY HIM FOR THE PRIVILEGE
> OF WHITEWASHING TOM
> SAT BY AND SAW THAT IT
> WAS WELL DONE.

This is patently untrue. Tom Sawyer never painted a fence in Hannibal, Missouri. There was never a gang of boys outside waiting in line to get a paintbrush.

Across the street is another false historical marker announcing:

> THIS WAS THE HOME OF BECKY
> THATCHER, TOM SAWYER'S FIRST
> SWEETHEART.

No, it was not.

A third sign sits down by the river:

> TOM SAWYER'S ISLAND
> IS SOUTHEAST FROM HERE
> ONE MILE DOWN THE RIVER.
> HERE HUCK FINN AND JIM STOPPED FOR A FEW DAYS
> ON THEIR WAY DOWN
> THE MISSISSIPPI.

Also false. Tom, Becky, Huck and Jim are fictional characters.

Hannibal, however, has decided to elide the boundary between literary representation and historical document, between fiction and fact. Twain, aka Sam Clemens, is an odd author on whom to base such a communal fantasy. He ends *The Adventures of Tom Sawyer* metafictionally playing with us: "So endeth this chronicle. It being strictly a history of a boy, it must stop here; the story could not go much further without becoming the history of a man. When one writes a novel about grown people, he knows exactly where to stop—that is, with a marriage; but when he writes of juveniles, he must stop where he best can."

Twain takes self-referentiality one step further in *The Adventures of Huckleberry Finn,* as if he felt compelled to wink harder. It opens this way:

PERSONS attempting to find a motive in this narrative will be prosecuted; persons attempting to find a moral in it will be banished; persons attempting to find a plot in it will be shot.

BY ORDER OF THE AUTHOR,
Per G.G., Chief of Ordnance.

But the City of Hannibal selectively ignores Twain's winks, erecting false idols to stories meant to exist only on a page. They have even preserved Becky Thatcher's house, and Huck's cabin. Or maybe they are one step ahead, taking tourists for suckers—a possible shout out to the tour guides in *Innocents Abroad,* Twain's novel about know-nothing Americans ineptly touring Europe, which is, of course, one step ahead of my own account of visiting Hannibal: "We find a piece of the true cross in every old church we go into, and some of the nails that held it together . . . I think we have seen as much as a keg of these nails. Then there is the crown of thorns; they have part of one in Sainte Chapelle, in Paris, and part of one, also, in Notre Dame. And as for bones of St. Denis, I feel certain we have seen enough of them to duplicate him if necessary."

Tourism is the third largest industry in Hannibal, behind agriculture and manufacturing; the top two of which bring in hardly any money. Hannibal would have withered away had it not been for its association with Mark Twain. And even with him, it is barely getting by. Apart from being home to Clemens for a few years, Hannibal is like so many other fly-over towns, living on the fumes of the plummeting industrial base. It looks much like the landscape of the rest of the country's rust belt: empty downtown storefronts, businesses with faded signs and "for sale" signs sprinkling residential lawns. The Rags to Riches Pawn Shop takes out a half-page ad in the *Hannibal Magazine* in which a pirate, wearing an eye patch and a parrot on his shoulder, holds open a treasure chest brimming with gold necklaces, bowls, goblets, and pearls. "Arrrrr! All yer worldly possessions right here

for your treasure hunting pleasures," the ad reads before brazenly admit-
ting: "We buy scrap gold!"

When I stopped in the store, Rags to Riches did not have pearls or
goblets. It did, however, have dozens of electric guitars and hundreds of
DVDs—the first things people unload, apparently, when things get tough.
Other shopping destinations in the "historic district" include Becky's Con-
signment Shop and Pudd'nhead's Antique Store. Inside both were items
destined to be the subject of the question "What do I do with this?" during
a basement spring-cleaning in a few years: items like St. Louis Cardinals
highball glasses, faux Norman Rockwell lithographs dotted with brown
stains, and model trains circa 1974. For lunch you can go to the Mark
Twain Dinette, where the signature dish is fried chicken and they make
their own root beer. Atop a flagpole sits a spinning sign in the shape of a
giant mug of the soft drink, brown in the middle and blue on the edges,
with the restaurant's name scrawled in light brown.

The historic district's offerings seem to exist solely for tourists. For
cough medicine—which I needed because Simon was coming down with a
cold—you have to leave downtown and drive up the hill to Mark Twain
Boulevard. I was sent to the Quik Stop at the Shell gas station about a mile
away.

Hannibal was not like my fantasy of it or of our mythic depictions of
small-town America. It is "America's Home Town" only if we expand our
definition of the term to encompass contradictions, too—if we approach it
as we might, say, a work of literature. Hannibal is not a postcard of iconic
American sweetness, not a Rockwell painting. It is at once snug and
smug—a place entirely familiar to me.

After I completed my dissertation, I got a teaching position at Oberlin
College. An elite liberal arts school with a great reputation (and also my
alma mater), Oberlin is a plum of a job. It is also in Oberlin, Ohio, a town
of 8,000 in Lorain County, thirty miles from Cleveland. Lorain County is
the second poorest county in Ohio, a state that has been struggling for
decades itself. I grew up in Madison, Wisconsin, and had already lived in
Oberlin as a student for four years, so I did not come with the coastal
prejudices against the Midwest and rural life that many of my colleagues
brought with them to their new academic jobs.

But I did not come with rosy platitudes about the virtues of small-town
America either. Sure, it is fun to run into people you know on the street,
but it is not fun to live in poverty. Nor do I patronize those who live here,

making them into victims, as do so many CNN stories about the "dying" heartland. This is where I live, not an anecdote. I find comfort and grit, but also a strain of know-nothing arrogance that rivals my own intellectual know-everything stance. To my coastal friends I defend where I live; to myself, I mutter frustration. If I do not want to set myself apart, then I must position myself as one of the family. Maybe I am the conflicted, alienated cousin who shows up grumpy to July 4th barbecues.

In his notebook, Twain noted that he was often asked, when traveling, if he was "an American." "No," he noted. "I am *the* American." Twain— uneducated, brilliant, entrepreneurial, adventuresome—has been made into an icon of "small-town" America. He is so only if we keep remembering that our small towns are complex. Twain relentlessly sought fame, and invested his fortune in a new printing technology that went belly-up. This is part of his small-town charm, too. He was also a scathing critic of any sort of ignorance, though he pilloried ignorance with good humor, never contempt.

Twain also treats Hannibal, or St. Petersburg acting as Hannibal, both sweetly and with cruelty in his work. Tom, who spends his entire life in St. Petersburg, exemplifies both strains of this dichotomy: in *The Adventures of Tom Sawyer*, he plays the lovable rapscallion; whereas in *Huckleberry Finn,* he's cruel and classist, looking down on Huck for his lowly status and, inhumanly, capturing Jim at the novel's end, knowing full well that the slave had already been freed. Huck, on the other hand, cannot be contained by the town; after returning from his adventures on the Mississippi, he flees once again, "because Aunt Sally she's going to adopt me and sivilize me, and I can't stand it. I been there before."

Twain never allowed Tom to grow up, because, once adult, he would "lie just like all the other one-horse men of literature and the reader would conceive a hearty contempt for him." Tom Sawyer stays within the world-view of a boy: he is honest—well nigh sincere—in the plain-speaking, straightforward way of boys. With Huck, the world is darker and more complex—its truth includes moral conviction as well as deceit, a sense that "to thine own self be true" can allow for befriending a slave and, at the same time, owning human chattel.

"Sivilizing" is what happens in St. Petersburg: schoolteachers are cruel, aunts make you take pain medicine, and slaves are whipped. But Twain uses the term to refer to St. Petersburg ironically. He portrays the town as hypocritical—cruelty masquerading as Christianity. The real heroes of the place are Huck and Jim, the boy the community refused to accept and would not educate, and the slave who tries to escape. Twain once defined a "real" civilization as a place that has none of the following: "human slavery, despotic government, inequality, numerous and brutal punishments for crimes, superstition almost universal, ignorance almost universal, and dirt and poverty almost universal." St. Petersburg had more than one of the above, so too does Hannibal—then and, one could argue, now.

You cannot enter the rooms inside the Mark Twain Boyhood Home. They are closed off, viewable only through Plexiglas. Behind the barriers, each room contains a ghostly white Mark Twain statue, circa age sixty, when he had the familiar visage from the iconic photographs, mustachioed and with mussed hair. Each sculpture is in a different pose: in one room he stands looking out a window, in another he sits at a table. Stiff and the color of drywall, each Twain is blindingly, disturbingly white. Behind the Twains are quotes from the author. The rest of the decoration in the rooms is period-era furniture.

"Look," I say to Simon. "Here's the kitchen. They didn't have stoves, so they cooked over a fire."

"Huh," he said, uninterested, and ran to the bedroom, which contains a second figure to complement the customary, creepy Stalin-esque statue. Behind a seated Twain is a rendering of a boy from behind, flat and in Plexiglas. He is looking out the window, with his hand raised, as if waving to someone outside.

"There's Tom Sawyer, waving to Huck," I tell my son, trying to keep him engaged. "He is trying to climb out the window."

Simon burst out of the room and ran outside of the house toward the place where the Tom cutout appears to be looking. It was by a stairway and Simon was leaning way, way, over the railing, peering curiously back at the house. "What are you doing?" I yelled to him.

"I want to see his face! I want to see what Tom looks like from the front!"

I wait for the results of his investigation. "Well?"

"It's blank. They didn't paint his face."

While Tom, Huck, and Becky signs and relics are everywhere in Hannibal, the town barely acknowledges Jim and Injun Joe, the villain in *The Adventures of Tom Sawyer*. I could only find one establishment named after Injun Joe, and—I kid you not—it is a campground. There are no Jim diners, no Jim pawn shops, no Jim amusement parks. I saw no historical markers making mention of Hannibal's slaveholding past. I didn't even see any blacks in my three days in the historic district. (As of the 2000 Census, 6.5 percent of Hannibal's population is African American, down from about 10 percent when Clemens lived there.)

During my tour of the Tom Sawyer Cave, a wonderful tour guide told us that *of course* Tom and Becky were never "really" in the cave, and Injun Joe did not starve to death inside. After I returned home, I read about the Injun Joe mentioned in the cave. There are actually two different characters named Injun Joe in Twain's work. One is a cruel criminal and the other was a harmless man who sometimes drank too much and entertained kids with stories. The latter seems to be a reference to a man named Joe Douglas, who some locals called Indian Joe, and who lived in Hannibal at around the same time as Clemens. Joe was a black man with some Native American blood and a well-known storyteller. He was also an upstanding citizen of the town and a respected property owner who always resented the confusion caused by Twain's character in *Tom Sawyer*.

Douglas is buried at Mt. Olivet cemetery, where some Clemens family members also were put to rest. About twenty years ago, the graveyard's caretaker wanted to draw more tourists, who might be curious as to the final resting place of the conniving Injun Joe. So he commissioned a headstone, which reads, in huge letters, INJUN JOE. Underneath is this inscription:

> Joe Douglass, known to many in Hannibal as "Indian Joe" died September 23 at age 102. He was found, an infant, in an abandoned Indian camp by a man named Douglass who raised him. He denied that he was the "Injun Joe" in Mark Twain's writings, as he had always lived an honorable life.

A real headstone to a real man (though his name is misspelled), labeled by the fictional name he hated, with an explanation below that the man buried there was actually nothing like his fictional counterpart? It sounds like a plot twist from *Pudd'nhead Wilson*.

In 1871, after working as steamboat pilot on the Mississippi, a reporter in Nevada, a printer in St. Louis, New York City, and Philadelphia, and assorted other jobs, and after marrying Olivia Langdon and having a son, Langdon, Clemens moved his family to Hartford, Connecticut. Langdon died at nineteen months. Clemens's daughter Suzy was born in 1872. In 1873, he commissioned an architect to design a new house. The Hartford home was a glorious marvel of whimsy—turrets and Victorian flourishes abound—and he hired Louis Comfort Tiffany and Associates to design the public rooms. Daughters Clara and Jean were born after they moved into the new house.

Twain's years in Hartford were the years his most famous novels were published: *The Adventures of Tom Sawyer, The Adventures of Huckleberry Finn, The Prince and the Pauper, Life on the Mississippi,* and *A Connecticut Yankee in King Arthur's Court.* Twain was a celebrity. And on first glance, the house befits a famous humor writer, capacious and whimsical. It is a showcase for irreverence.

But Twain wrote very little in the Hartford house. He found it distracting. He abandoned the room originally intended for his study for another room above the coach house. Dissatisfied with that room's cramped quarters, he moved his desk to the billiard room on the third floor. He covered the table with books during the day and removed them at night to play pool. But he ended up doing most of his writing at his sister-in-law's house in Elmira, in upstate New York.

Twain was always interested in the production of writing—he worked as a printer when he was young, and while in Hartford he invested in the Paige Compositor, an automatic typesetting machine. But the company failed, taking with it most of his savings.

Struck by tragedy and money troubles, he eventually had to leave the Hartford house. In 1894, he declared bankruptcy. In 1896, his daughter Suzy died in the house while Twain was away giving lectures in Europe. Her death sent Twain into a serious depression. He never set foot in the house again. He wrote: "To us our house was not unsentient matter—it had a heart & a soul & eyes to see us with, & approvals & solicitudes & deep sympathies; it was of us, & we were in its confidence, & lived in its grace & in the peace of its benediction. We never came home from an absence that its face did not light up & speak out its eloquent welcome—& we could not enter it unmoved."

In 1903 the president of the Hartford Fire Insurance Company moved into the house. In 1917, it became a school for boys. Then it was used to store coal, and after that, it was divided up into apartments. In 1929, the Mark Twain Memorial Committee bought it.

Today, the Twain house in Hartford is beautiful, well maintained, and well run by a private foundation. On display is an old Paige compositor as well as a seven and a half foot Lego Mark Twain House. You can follow the "TwainHouse" on Twitter, join its Facebook group, and read its blog. Flocks of school kids take tours.

But if you know how Twain felt when he left the house, if you know the various reduced uses the house was put to after his death—a storehouse for coal?—if you look at the Paige compositor and think of all that unfulfilled hope and all those lost dollars, the place is pretty darned bittersweet, despite all the great Twain quips the tour guide provides as you wander about.

The Hartford house is an architectural and literary homage to irony. Unlike Hannibal, it is never straight. But in the Hartford house I found little to laugh at, in spite of the guide's relentless upbeat patter, the fun on display everywhere. In Hannibal I think only of Twain's ironic insights and capacity for play; in Hartford I think of his sadness and vulnerability. They are all mixed up, my emotions: snide in Hannibal, chastened in Hartford.

Despite Twain's status as an iconic, defining American writer—a title well-earned if based upon his trenchant ability to limn our national character—Twain was always both of this place and not at all. He mocks Americans, shows us our foibles, and is far too introspective for any plainspoken, up-by-the-bootstraps innocence. His house museums cannot get him right, but you cannot blame them for trying. Their misreadings are poignant. And Twain, as always, is one step ahead of us. I imagine Twain would laugh uproariously at our attempts to preserve him. In 1906, he was asked to speak publicly against an attempt to fill in "Tom Sawyer's cave." "I had nothing to say," he recalls in his autobiography. "I was sorry we lost our cement mine but it was not worth while to talk about it at this late day and, to take it all around, it was a painful subject anyway."

I imagine how scathing his essay on visiting the new restored cave and Mark Twain houses would be if he were alive to experience them and write about it. Maybe the title would be something like *Innocents at Home*—a sequel to *Innocents Abroad*. I picture him chuckling to himself in Elmira, yet another house in which he lived, and one in which he was most productive. I laugh just thinking about his reaction to those plaster statues of himself in the Hannibal home. But then the tape keeps rolling and I imagine him later that night. He is alone in bed, tossing and turning. The act of writing has brought up for him memories of cruelty and poverty and death, of all the sorrows that his houses enshrine. I do not want to find a one-to-one correlation between thing and idea. I want to find something that resists, that defies expectations, and that portrays contradictions, not causation. I do not want to dip my hand in the same Mississippi Twain swam in. With the utmost respect for Borges, that strikes me as a markedly unTwainian sentimentality.

We check out of the motel in Hannibal and Simon tells me, in the unbelievably sincere tone of a nine-year-old, that he had a really good time. I sling our bags in the trunk of the rental car, relieved to be going home, and head downriver to the airport. I cherish my son's credulity. Heck, he wants to believe the tooth fairy exists, even though he knows I leave the money under his pillow. But he is nine, and, like Tom Sawyer, has yet to enter the age of irony. The town of Hannibal, though, is old enough to know better. Once you are grown-up, sincerity needs to be harder fought.

The Alcotts' Orchard House

Chapter 4

The Concord Pilgrimage

> The use of literature is to afford us a platform whence we
> may command a view of our present life, a purchase by
> which we may move it. We fill ourselves with ancient
> learning, install ourselves the best we can in Greek, in Punic,
> in Roman houses, only that we may wiselier see French,
> English, and American houses and modes of living. In like
> manner, we see literature best from the midst of wild
> nature, or from the din of affairs, or from a high religion.
> The field cannot be well seen from within the field.
>
> —Ralph Waldo Emerson, "Circles"

> The Concord pilgrimage should be one of the most fruitful
> and beneficent of human experiences. Familiarity with the
> physical stand-point of our authors, with the scenes amid
> which they lived and wrote, and with the objects which
> suggested the imagery of their poems, the settings of their
> tales, and which gave tone and color to their work, will
> not only bring us into closer sympathy with the writers,
> but will help us to a better understanding of the writings.
> —Theodore Wolfe, "A Concord Pilgrimage"

IT IS TEMPTING to dismiss Hannibal as an example of philistine American-
ism, but as Twain himself makes clear in *Innocents Abroad*, European literary tourism can be shlocky and historically sketchy, too. I went to the Dante
house in Florence, which is arguably the house dedicated to the earliest
Western writer (Petrarch runs a close second), only discover a house that
Dante never lived in, and one that is not even medieval—it was built in the
nineteenth century to look like a medieval house. It is filled with yellowing
dry-mounted posters, a dusty apothecary display, and a model of Rome
with little bulbs that light up when you push buttons. The guide they sell
at the ticket booth says of the reconstructed bedroom, "this was certainly
not Dante's bedroom."

The house is mentioned on many "Florence in a day" bus and buggy
tours, and as I hung out in the plaza outside the house I heard guides tromp
through the street and say "Casa di Dante" to their groups, but barely slow
down. The house is off a shopping street, so many tourists carrying recent
purchases in logo-strewn bags pass by as well. "Casa di Dante," they invari-
ably say back and forth say to one another as they walk by (admittedly, it
is quite fun to say "Casa di Dante"). But few linger, and fewer enter. If you
do go inside, as did I, you will see a diorama of a medieval battle with toy
soldiers on toy horseback facing off. You will learn about the florin, the
currency of Dante's day, and see big fake florins next to one tiny real one,
both in front of an illustration of bankers. You will see the apothecary
display, filled with dried herbs on branches and herbs ground up in a mor-
tar and pestle. Coats of arms are displayed throughout the three-story
house.

Of course, we know less about this author than many who have come
since, so it is harder to figure out exactly what to display, but still, the Casa

di Dante is about as unsophisticated as a museum can be—it's more like a fourth-grade history fair on medieval Florence. Fittingly, most of the visitors to the house are Florentine kids on school field trips.

The Schiller house in Marbach, Germany, was home to the author only until he was four, and the family only lived in one room. There is no proof that Anne Hathaway's cottage is where Shakespeare courted his future wife. However, these sites have been around for so long that they have a history too, and thus an authenticity acquired by years of visits. For example, the windowpane in the Shakespeare Birthplace, which may not be where Shakespeare was born, bears the signatures of Thomas Carlyle and Charles Dickens, who etched their names on the glass to mark their presence in the house. Even *Innocents Abroad* records an authentic history, the nineteenth-century hucksters who sold gullible American tourists faux relics.

If American authors are your thing, you would think the place to visit would be New York City, the literary center of the United States. However, that is not the case for literary tourism, and certainly not for writers' houses. *Novel Destinations: Literary Landmarks from Jane Austen's Bath to Ernest Hemingway's Key West* includes hundreds of literary lodgings, walking tours, museums, restaurants and parks as well as houses associated with British and American novelists. New York is hardly mentioned. There is an entry for St. Patrick's Cathedral, where F. Scott and Zelda Fitzgerald were married, and the Plaza Hotel, where they drank. The Chelsea Hotel and the Algonquin are mentioned based on their hosting of authors, and McSorley's, the White Horse Tavern and Chumley's for bars associated with writers. The New York Public Library gets a mention. But not much beyond that. There is only one writers' house museum in New York, the Poe Cottage in the Bronx. (Marianne Moore's Greenwich Village living room was moved, and you can view it on the third floor of the Rosenbach museum in Philadelphia.)

New York is the America of striving, moving, and restlessness. Writers' houses preserve domesticity. Not a good match. In fact, it is a suburb that is ground zero for writers' houses in America: Concord, Massachusetts. Over two hundred published writers call this small town home, and it is full of writers' house museums—five in all. The town has been bringing tourists in to see these homes as far back as the 1840s, when the writers were still alive. Then, the Transcendentalist greats, Ralph Waldo Emerson, Henry David Thoreau, Bronson Alcott, and his daughter Louisa, all lived nearby, friends and neighbors, going back and forth from each others' houses, and entertaining visiting literary tourists. By 1895, it was considered "another Stratford" that "attracts more pilgrims than any other place of equal size upon the continent . . . to which come reverent pilgrims from the Old World and the New to worship at its shrines and to wander through the scenes hallowed by the memories of its illustrious *littérateurs,* seers, and evangels."

For those who buy into literary idolatry, writers' houses serve as secular shrines, places where one believes a miracle occurred—the penning of a masterpiece, the birth of a genius. People trek to pilgrimage sites because they believe that it will strengthen their faith to pay homage in person. The house—or the typewriter or the desk or the chair—is the mediating fetish object. Inside the house—or looking at the typewriter or sitting on the porch—one experiences a moment of calm, of meditation, that is spiritual. Borges wants to dip his hand in Twain's Mississippi, a spiritual spring, to pay homage, but for many more, Concord is the source of American genius, and in the town writers' houses are, well, a cottage industry.

So I went to Concord, begrudgingly. I never fell prey to that certain cult of Transcendentalism that so animates many Americans, often beginning in adolesence among the male of our species, and often accompanied by another form of American secular worship, to nature (in college we called these types "Nature Boys," with their shaggy hair and frequent walks in the arboretum to commune with trees and birds.) To me, though, the Transcendentalists seemed very far off in time and style, and always a bit too Protestant. But who could argue with the astoundingly literary output this coterie of friends produced? Many consider Bloomsbury an icon of a writers-and-friends community, but Concord in the mid-nineteenth century rivals the Bloomsbury group for intense personal and professional interchanges.

I arrived in Concord sweaty—it was Labor Day weekend—and exhausted. I had driven twelve hours straight with my friend Jane, who dropped me off on her way to visit friends in Boston. I was not looking forward to the weekend. I was tired in advance thinking about how very many houses there were to visit: Emerson's house, Orchard House, The Wayside, The Old Manse, and of course the site of Thoreau's cabin near Walden Pond. I had my hackles up in advance, expecting a certain on-high self-righteousness in town. Before the trip I read about how Thoreau—who alone among the biggies at Concord was born here—believed that Concord was "a

microcosm 'by the study of which the whole world could be comprehended.'" He rarely left town. Bronson Alcott quipped that Thoreau
thought "he dwelt in the centre of the universe, and seriously contemplated
annexing the rest of the planet to Concord."

I had booked a room at the Concord Colonial Inn, a down-at-heels
lodge that is both charming and slightly tattered in a New England sort of
way. The building dates to 1716, with additions from the 1970s. For lunch
you can order cornbread, chicken potpies, lobster rolls, and Yankee pot
roast. I thought it would be appropriate to be car-less in Concord. I would
do some Thoreauvian walking. I underestimated the distances, though, and
brought the wrong shoes, so trekking back and forth along the Lexington
Highway made me uncomfortable and grouchy. I told myself I was experi-
encing a slight sense of deprivation I could call ruggedly Transcendental.

The first house I visited was the Emerson house. I chose it because I
wanted to give Emerson—arguably the most important of the entire Concord crowd and an Oz-like figure to the others—his due. Emerson supported all the other famous writers in this town. He paid the rent for
Hawthorne, slipped the Alcotts cash, and let Thoreau live in his house for
years. His works, among the Concord legacy, are arguably the most
astoundingly original and nation shaping, though they are the least read
today. Emerson, who was deemed both the "sage of Concord" and "Concord itself," lived here for years. He chose Concord because, as a poet, he
believed he "must therefore live in the country; a sunset, a forest, a river
view are more to me than many friends." So he left Boston for Concord,
and wrote of his move, "Good-by, proud world! I'm going home."

Here is what Theodore Wolfe saw when he went to Concord for his
book, *Literary Shrines*:

> Behind a row of dense-leaved horse-chestnuts ranged along the
> highway, the quondam home of Emerson nestles among clustering
> evergreens which were planted by Bronson Alcott and Henry D.
> Thoreau for their friend. A copse of pines sighs in the summer wind
> close by; an orchard planted and pruned by Emerson's hands, and a
> garden tended by Thoreau, extend from the house to a brook flowing
> through the grounds and later joining the Concord by the famous old
> Manse; beyond the brook lies the way to Walden. . . . The mansion is
> a substantial, square, clapboarded structure of two stories, with hip-
> roofs; a square window projects at one side; a wing is joined at

the back; covered porches protect the entrances; light paint covers the plain walls which gleam through the bowering foliage, and the whole aspect of the place is delightfully attractive and home-like.

When he lived there, Emerson's house was a hub, a destination. "To these plain rooms as to an intellectual court came, from his own and other lands, hundreds famed in art, literature, and politics. Here came Curtis and Bartol . . . John Brown, Whittier, Agassiz, Longfellow, Lowell, . . . Whitman, Harte, James," Wolfe writes. Behind them were the first penitents, the Nature Boys of the antebellum age: "With these came another class of pilgrims, the great army of impracticables—men with long hair, long beards, long collars,— each intent upon securing the endorsement of Emerson for his own pet scheme." When Theodore Wolfe visited, an Emerson still lived there, his "unmarried daughter—of saint-like face and nun-like garb [who] inhabits his home and cherishes its treasures."

When I visited, a tour guide opened the door for me. The place is only open for a few hours a day, and each visitor is greeted at the door. The tour began in the library. Our guide asked me and the others to sit. A family of four, tourists, with two teenaged girls—one looked interested, the other bored—sat on the red velvet sofa. I chose the faded pink corner chair. The guide stood at the front of the room and started. It was like a presentation for her college class: she had memorized a script. She looked beyond us, out the window, trying to remember what she was supposed to say next. She tripped up a few times, getting dates and names wrong. I thought about raising my hand and asking clarifying questions, but decided against it. I was taking notes, and I think I made her nervous.

We were allowed to sit on the furniture because the real furniture is across the street at the Concord Museum. The room we were in was a replica, with a replica of the circular table, at which Emerson wrote. He kept his journals in the real table's drawers. His journal was, he said, his "savings bank," because he could withdraw from it when he needed to. Replica bookshelves line the entire far wall, and replica wheat-looking wall-paper pops from behind the fireplace. There is a guest register on the windowsill.

Emerson finished writing "Nature" in this room (he began it in the Old Manse, on the other side of town), and lived in this house for forty-six years. The Emerson family still owns the place, and they keep some of his nonreplicated stuff here: his walking sticks, his dressing gown, and his hat, which sits on a peg in the foyer. I stared long and hard at Emerson's hat on that peg, and, I must admit, felt chills.

Halfway through our tour a new guide took over. This one was chirpy and put together: she wore a black pencil skirt, sensible pumps, a blue and white striped sweater, and prominently displayed on her chest was a gold cross encrusted with tiny colored stones. She had also memorized her script, but was more experienced, or simply better at her job. She could talk to us and still maintain eye contact.

In the hallway were some chairs that she told us were from the dining room set. One of the set, she said, was made by Henry David Thoreau for his friend and benefactor. It contained a drawer underneath the seat. Emerson was always late for church because he could never find his gloves, and Thoreau put the drawer in so "now Emerson would have no excuse, because his gloves were always in the drawer." (Later, I read that that drawer was actually made for Mrs. Emerson. I don't know who is right. Either way, Thoreau seems to have been the carpenter, and it makes a good tour anecdote.)

In the parlor, a portrait of Carlyle hangs. Below it is Carlyle's signature, which Emerson cut out from a piece of correspondence and pasted below the portrait. I stared at it for a long time, imagining Emerson's desire to show others, to display his literary connections. The guide then showed us a Julia Cameron photograph of Carlyle. At this point in the tour, I realized that some of this was worth quite a bit of change. Upstairs, in the master bedroom, off in an alcove, was a 1700s flat-top highboy. I imagined the furniture appraisers Leslie and Leigh Keno from *Antiques Roadshow*, jumping up and down with excitement as if they were on the tour with me. In the master bedroom, we also learned the origin of the phrase "sleep tight"—a rope bed was used to keep the strings underneath the mattress taut. We looked at the pegs that ropes were affixed to and all went "huh" as the guide explained them to us.

But the house is not set up like a glitzy historic house showplace. In the nursery was a glass display cabinet. Inside it were dusty curios and knick-knacks labeled with typewritten three-by-five cards that were cut down to size. These objects, forgotten and uncurated, are probably worth a lot of money. The whole place epitomizes Yankee shabby gentility.

Upstairs the guides switched places again, and we were left with the first one, the one wearing white slippers and goofing up her script. She showed us the other Julia Cameron photograph, this one of Tennyson and the Daniel Chester French bust of Emerson (French also did the Lincoln Memorial). Of the bust, Emerson remarked, the guide told us: "This is indeed the face that I shave every morning." Again, a snappy little tour anecdote that made the group giggle.

After the tour, I asked who operated the house only to discover that it is about the most opaque writers' house museum in terms of maintenance and financing. Old money, again. The Ralph Waldo Emerson Memorial Association runs it, and you can only discuss its maintenance and financing with the president, Margaret Emerson Bancroft, a relative of Emerson, if you write her a letter.

The house's aura of New England aristocracy gives it a grace that sits well with Emersonianism. The disjuncture between the author's literature, his beliefs, his chosen way of life, and the house itself seems small. The museum fits the museumed, like the hat haphazardly sitting on the peg by the back door.

Which is why one should probably not do as I did, and visit the Concord Museum after leaving the Emerson house. Across the street there is an eerie repetition of what you have just seen.

The Concord Museum is where Emerson's nonreplica study is. Or, rather, the *real* study is a fake. However you parse it, it's spooky. You see the stuff all over again, staged exactly the same way as it is in the house: that same circular table, corner chair, sofa, and wheaty wallpaper. A scant hour after I had sat in the library in the house, I peered at its "authentic" twin from behind glass in the Concord Museum.

I pressed a button and heard the voices of people; actors read quotations from famous people about their experiences in the study, and you can listen to them on loop tape. You can stand there for a long time, as I did, asking yourself, "Which is more real?" "Which is more authentic?" "Which best captures a moment in Emerson's life?" It is, like the words spoken aloud as you stand there musing, thoughts on a loop tape, recursive and unanswerable. Emerson writes in "Circles": "Every ultimate fact is only the first of a new series. Every general law only a particular fact of some more general law presently to disclose itself. There is no outside, no inclosing wall, no circumference to us. The man finishes his story,—how good! how final! how it puts a new face on all things! He fills the sky. Lo! on the other side rises also a man, and draws a circle around the circle we had just pronounced the outline of the sphere. Then already is our first speaker not man, but only a first speaker. His only redress is forthwith to draw a circle outside of his antagonist. And so men do by themselves."

After a long lunch break on the porch of the Colonial Inn, it was time to suck it up and go to Walden Pond. I had tried to leave this out of my study of writers' house museums, as there is no preserved house per se. Also, of course, it was not a house Thoreau happened to live in, but a place he famously built in order to live deliberately. But my reasons against it were weak. There had been a house, after all, and the site of the tiny cabin in which Thoreau wrote *Walden* is marked off. Plus, it is the ultimate literary pilgrimage site in the United States.

It was early Sunday morning, not so hot, and beautifully clear—the last day of August, the day before Labor Day, the last day of summer. I had blisters from my walks to the Emerson House the day before, so when I bought my muffin at the Market Café I asked the server if there was a place I could rent a bike. She said no. The woman behind me in line offered to give me a ride to Walden, as it was on her way home.

She dropped me off at a very busy intersection right before the Walden Pond State Park and I stood for a while, waiting for the light to change so I could cross. When I got into the park, there were no signs pointing me to the cabin site. I saw some pathways of desire—paths tromped by others—so I followed them through the woods, winding my way down to the pond itself, before seeing a small wooden sign and walking back up the bank to the site.

There, a family of Japanese tourists was taking pictures. The dad told the son, who was playing with the chain draped around the ghost of the cabin's original floor plan, to stop. There is no cabin, of course, at Walden Pond. There are chains marking off empty space. In the middle of the ground where the house was is a plaque.

I checked my email on my cell phone (the reception was fine), and sat by a tree to take notes. It really was very beautiful, and calm, and soothing, sitting there, leaning against the tree, watching kids swim in the pond, and noting the passers-by. An elderly, rail-thin man in boxer shorts and mumbling to himself stumbled past. He was followed by a middle-aged man, yelling to his wife in Spanish about finding a good spot, before changing into his swimsuit, using his towel to cover himself in that European (read: un-American) way.

Walden Pond still receives the most visitors of all the literary sites in

Concord, Always has. But then again, it is also a nice place to swim. By World War I, thirty thousand pilgrims were visiting Walden Pond a year. By the 1970s, that number was half a million. The road to Walden gets taken enough that it has earned its own nomenclature and rituals. The Thoreauvian pilgrimage follows the structure of the Christian pilgrimage: "All sites of pilgrimage have this in common: they are believed to be places where miracles once happened, still happen, and may happen again. Even where the time of miraculous healings is reluctantly conceded to be past, believers firmly hold that faith is strengthened and salvation better secured by personal exposure to the beneficent unseen presence of the Blessed Virgin or the local saint, mediated through a cherished image or painting." As Lawrence Buell has brilliantly written, the Thoreauvian pilgrimage follows religious suit: the site is rendered "in an atmosphere of holy calm," pilgrims reenact a journey, and they leave with relics.

By 1863, only one year after Thoreau's death, Walden was transformed into a sacred place. Thoreau died young, at age forty-four, and so in death became even more of a Romantic figure. People who knew Thoreau were leery of visiting Walden Pond while others were there lounging and enjoying the view. Thoreau himself had welcomed "all honest pilgrims, who came out of the woods for freedom's sake, and really left the village behind." But his friends wanted to visit while it was quiet, to feel his presence solitarily.

Emerson took Bret Harte to Walden Pond in 1871. Harte joked about how close this natural retreat was to town: "so close to civilization that one could be called into dinner upon any occasion." The Thoreauvian pilgrimage, as Buell notes, would always conveniently omit the nearby traffic, the crowds, and the pond's one-mile distance from the center of Concord.

That people liked to hang out and relax at Walden Pond kept disturbing purists. In 1872, a guidebook, *The Woods and By-Ways of New England*, written by Wilson Flagg, lamented that "Every student of nature or admirer of poetry . . . should make a visit to Walden Pond" and "seek the spot." Such pilgrims were contributing to "the present desecration of that hallowed spot by making it the ground for picnics—assemblages of people who go there, not for the observation of nature, but for ice creams and soda water." But remember: even when Thoreau was living there, he invited people to stop by for a visit. It was only after his death that everyone complained that the place was what it never had been: a quiet, sacred chapel.

While there was no monument to Thoreau, people did want to have something, something material, to mark the spot. On one occasion, Bronson Alcott was taking a walk with a friend at Walden. They discussed the lack of memorial, and Bronson said that a monument did not seem appropriate. So they decided to build a cairn. Cairns are a tradition from Scotland and Wales, wherein people leave stones to honor great men and the stones would build into piles proportional to the greatness of the deceased. Mary Newberry Adams, the friend of Alcott, wrote her name on a stone and left it there. As Bronson wrote, "The rude stones were a monument more fitting than the costliest carving of the artist." So from then on, pilgrims would leave something on the spot of the cabin instead of taking something away.

By 1876 there was a sign, "Site of Thoreau's Hut," by the cairn. In the 1880s, Bronson Alcott's Concord School of Philosophy held tours of historic spots in Concord. By then, any Thoreauvian would expect the same ritual: a walk from town to the pond, there to find the cairn, leave a stone, and walk back to town.

It is funny to think of people hawking wares at Walden Pond, as happened when E. B. White walked to Walden Pond. He wrote about his experience in 1939 (addressing Thoreau):

> I knew I must be nearing your woodland retreat when the Golden Pheasant lunchroom came into view—Sealtest ice cream, toasted sandwiches, hot frankfurters, waffles, tonics. . . . Beyond the Pheasant was a place called Walden Breezes . . . Behind the Breezes, in a sun parched clearing, dwelt your philosophical descendants in their trailers . . . Cushman's bakery truck had stopped to deliver an early basket of rolls. . . . Leaving the highway I turned off into the woods toward the pond, which was apparent through the foliage. . . . From beneath the flattened popcorn wrapper (*granum explusum*) peeped the frail violet . . . [there were] dressing rooms for swimmers, a float with diving towers, drinking fountains of porcelain, and rowboats for hire.

In 1945, on July 4, a group of Thoreauvians met to memorialize one century from the day Thoreau moved into the cabin. One of them was Roland Wells Robbins, who was not educated but wanted to be a writer. At the ceremony, people started to debate where the actual cabin had been. Robbins started researching. Then digging. And in October, he finally found plaster under the dirt. He had found the remains of the cabin.

To honor the discovery, they put up nine granite posts, mined from the farm where Thoreau was born. In 1985, Robbins built a replica of the cabin. It is near the parking lot, not at the original site, confusing many pilgrims.

Today, the Commonwealth of Massachusetts maintains Walden. Occasionally, they close it down so the natural ecology does not suffer too much damage. There have been intense political battles over how much of the woods should be open to the public and how much should be preserved. In 1990, musician Don Henley of the Eagles started The Walden Woods Project to preserve the area around the pond. He has raised millions of dollars toward his goal. Bill and Hillary Clinton visited in 1998 to see his work.

I never went to the replica house. Nor did I leave a stone at Walden. But I did spend a long time admiring how the new cairn is growing.

What separates the Thoreauvian pilgrimage from other acts of secular devotion at a writer's house is that at Walden one leaves something, whereas at many other places one takes something away—a souvenir, like the magnets that populate my fridge, or the stuffed Herman Melville, holding a whale and a copy of *Bartleby,* that sits on my window sill. Or, simply, a story to tell.

If we extend the analogy to the act of reading, ideally one leaves a part of oneself in a book, not the other way around. For me, reading is an act of absorption—"immersion in, raptness in, engrossment in, occupation with, preoccupation with, engagement in, captivation with, fascination with, enthrallment with," as the thesaurus puts it. All too often, people feel compelled to "get something from" reading, to make it transactional, an exchange benefitting only the reader. For me, it is the act of giving, of leaving myself that I always fervently strive for when reading. I am troubled by our contemporary insistence on reading as a vehicle for self-identification, for gobbling up literature in the image of ourselves. I would rather leave myself at the doorstep of a book, give the work power over me, and offer myself to it. What I value about reading is its capacity to create self-abnegation. As Emerson put it, "The one thing which we seek with insatiable desire is to forget ourselves, to be surprised out of our propriety, to lose our sempiternal memory, and to do something without knowing how or why; in short, to draw a new circle."

This, of course, is a very religious desire, an act of supplication. It is not unlike leaving a stone. Which is why I do not know why I did not add to the cairn, other than some residual, stubborn arrogance at any form of hero-worship. In "Representative Men" Emerson tells us that "it is natural to believe in great men. . . . The search for the great is the dream of youth, and the most serious occupation of manhood. We travel into foreign parts to find his works, if possible, to get a glimpse of him." I am, it seems, either unnatural or unserious. Or preternaturally anti-Concordian.

Hungry, and lacking a ride home, I decided to walk back to the Inn, all one mile of it, feeling the blisters. Once back in town, I went to a café and had a lobster roll.

Thoreau went off to be by himself and write, and this view of authorship is consonant with many of our myths: the most common cultural image recalled with the phrase "the author" is the Romantic genius, alone, in a garret (or hut), writing furiously, crumpling up papers and throwing them on the floor, losing track of time, heedless of the public, obsessed with his own imagination. In this archetypal scene, the author is anything but domestic.

A common cultural image of domesticity is a house, children, mother, father, and a hearth. Perhaps the children are seated on the parlor floor, listening to their father tell a story. Or they are cavorting in snow in the front of a well-lit house while mother prepares dinner and father reads. In the American popular imagination, the novel that most typifies this domestic scene is Louisa May Alcott's *Little Women*. But here is a funny thing: if anyone could be said to have really written in a garret, alone and oblivious, it is Alcott. A passage from *Little Women* that is largely autobiographical is almost a parody of the Romantic artist cliché. Here, Jo, the character who most resembles Alcott, describes writing:

> Every few weeks she would shut herself up in her room, put on her scribbling suit, and "fall into a vortex," as she expressed it, writing away at her novel with all her heart and soul, for till that was finished she could find no peace. . . . When the writing fit came on, she gave herself up to it with entire abandon, and held a blissful life, unconscious of want, care, or bad weather, while she sat safe and happy in an imaginary world, full of friends almost as real and dear to her as any in the flesh. Sleep forsook her eyes, meals stood untasted, day and night were all too short to enjoy the happiness

which blessed her only at such times. . . . The divine afflatus usually lasted a week or two, and then she emerged from her "vortex" hungry, sleepy, cross, or despondent.

Alcott, the woman who most Americans associate with domesticity, exemplified the romanticism of the tortured artist. Why is our image of her so dissonant with her actual experience?

Little Women is fairly autobiographical, but the differences between Alcott's life and the novel are crucial. To name a few: Alcott never married, and Jo does. Alcott wrote her whole life, mainly penning commercial work she would have preferred not to write, because she had to support her sick mother and financially challenged father, Bronson. The novel she most wanted to succeed was *Moods*, her first work, and a philosophical, metaphysical novel. Jo, on the other hand, becomes a teacher at a boys' school. Bronson Alcott, a vegan who once swore off wool because he didn't want to offend the sheep, was an influential but comical figure—a Transcendentalist who cast an enormous shadow over Louisa's life and who relied on others, including Emerson and his daughter Louisa, to support him. He was renowned for hanging out on a bench outside his house eager to chat with any passersby. His neighbor, Nathaniel Hawthorne, wrote a poem about him:

> There lived a Sage at Appleslump
> Whose dinner never made him plump;
> Give him carrots, potatoes, squash, turnips and peas,
> And a handful of crackers without any cheese,
> And a cup of cold water to wash down all these,
> And he'd prate of the Piritit as long as you please,
> This airy Sage of Appleslump.

Mr. March, on the other hand, valiantly fights in the Civil War and, once he returns, nicely fades into the background.

Finally, the Alcott family, from Louisa's birth to death, was, to most of middle-class mainstream America, a bunch of weirdo radicals, who supported John Brown, progressive education, and women's rights. When Louisa wrote a poem that expressed support for Brown, to be read at the Annual Concord School Exhibition, the elders of Concord, whom Louisa considered conservative and called "Old Fogies," refused to read the poem aloud. Her mother denounced the town's conservatism as well. In other words, the Alcotts were anything but the idealized American family enshrined by the founders of the Orchard House museum.

Louisa's adult life is a story of her struggle to balance the sometimes oppressive needs of her family—represented by her life in Orchard House—with her desire to live independently and write whatever she wanted to.

When Louisa was twenty-nine and the Civil War came, she wanted to go off and become a soldier. Unable to fight, she served as a nurse. She came down with typhoid, and the doctors tried to cure her with calumel, which contains mercury. She would suffer the rest of her life with the effects of mercury poisoning. After her monomaniacal vortices, she would become so fatigued she would be ill for months.

But she wrote nonetheless, for her writing was the main source of money for herself and her parents after her sisters all moved out of the house. Louisa, who always envisaged for herself what Jo also wanted—an independent life—was the one stuck at home taking care of her aging parents. In 1866, when her mother, Abba, was quite ill, Bronson went to give lectures in St. Louis and visit friends. Louisa stayed with Abba and wrote to pay the bills.

When Jo is left in the house after her sisters marry off, she reflects on her fate:

> Poor Jo! These were dark days to her, for something like despair came over her when she thought of spending all her life in that quiet house, devoted to hum-drum cares, a few poor little pleasures, and the duty that never seemed to grow any easier. "I can't do it. I wasn't meant for a life like this, and I know I shall break away and do something desperate if somebody don't come and help me," she said to herself, when her first efforts failed, and she fell into the moody, miserable state of mind which often comes when strong wills have to yield to the inevitable.

When Alcott finally earned enough money to keep everyone afloat, she moved out of Orchard House, and Concord. She rented herself a room in Boston. She called this room "Gamp's Garrett," a reference to *Martin Chuzzlewit*. There, she wrote an essay called "Happy Women," in 1868, which offers an ironic slant on her famous novel's title. In it, she tells young girls that, "liberty is a better husband than love to many of us" and discusses "the loss of happiness and self-respect that comes with an ill considered marriage." Then she profiled women who chose to remain single, "superior" women. She called them: a doctor, a missionary, a music teacher, and an author based upon herself.

When her mother fell ill again, Alcott was forced to move back home. At the time, her publisher suggested she write a book for girls. She did not want to. "I don't enjoy this sort of thing," she said. "Never liked girls or knew many, except my sisters."

Alcott finally decided to write the novel, and set off to create a tale of girls who subscribed to the Alcottian ideals of self-sacrifice and familial duty, but also strove for independence and to succeed at whatever endeavor they most desired, be it traditionally feminine and domestic, as with Meg and Beth, who want to marry and tend house, respectively, or more unconventional, as with Amy and Jo, who want to become artists.

After Alcott published part I of *Little Women*, she received letters from girls who loved the book. But most were anxious to know whom the girls would marry. Would Jo marry the dashing Laurie? They could only hope. Alcott's publishers insisted she do so, but she did not want Jo to marry anyone. Eventually, she compromised, and made for Jo a "funny match," as she put it, with the older, intellectual Professor Bhaer.

In the novel, when Jo is in the bleak mood created by one of her vortices, she decides that she would not marry. " 'An old maid—that's what I'm to be. A literary spinster, with a pen for a spouse, a family of stories for children, and twenty years hence a morsel of fame, perhaps when . . . I'm old, and can't enjoy it—solitary, and can't share it, independent, and don't need it. Well, I needn't be a sour saint nor a selfish sinner; and, I dare say, old maids are very comfortable when they get used to it; but—'and there Jo sighed, as if the prospect was not inviting."

Alcott kept writing about the March family in the many sequels to *Little Women*. In *Jo's Boys*, she makes the school Jo teaches at, Plumfield, coeducational, and limns her views of women's rights more forcefully. A college is added to Plumfield that admits all, regardless of race or religion. Nan, the first girl student at Plumfield, refuses advances from a boy and stays unmarried, happily so, and becomes a doctor.

Jo's Boys was written fifteen years after *Little Women*, and Alcott could not wait to be done with the Marches. In one chapter, Jo asks for privacy as scores of admirers come to her house to find pieces of her. One asks her to pen her name to his book. One wants a pair of her stockings to make into a rug. Her publisher wanted her to take out the chapter, but Alcott responded that she wanted to tell people "not to harass the authors whom they hold in their regard." She felt her readers had reduced Jo, and by proxy Alcott, to "a literary nurse-maid who provides moral pap for the young."

Still, readers continue to cast Jo as a young, spirited sprite. Alcott complained, "Why people will think Jo small when she is described as tall I don't see, and why insist that she must be young when she is said to be 30 at the end of the book?"

The success of *Little Women* made Alcott the most famous woman author in America. People started to visit Concord to get a glimpse of her, and "reporters haunt the place to look at the authoress, who dodges into the woods." To avoid them, she moved back to Boston. When she returned to Concord the next spring, she was "annoyed by the intrusions of the . . . . curious who had mistaken her for an exhibit."

Another reason our view of Alcott is sentimentalized is that Orchard House was made into a museum only a few years after her death, and the organizers of the museum created it as a shrine to domesticity.

In America, historic preservation began as woman's work. One of the first acts of historic preservation in America was making Mount Vernon into a museum. That job was undertaken in 1858 by the Mount Vernon Ladies Association and became a model for subsequent house museums. That a group of volunteer women were granted legitimacy to complete this project "confirmed that the rescue of 'sacred' historic houses was within the proper, domestically based 'sphere' of woman's activity," as Patricia West puts it in *Domesticating History: The Political Origins of America's House Museums*. Orchard House was preserved in the spirit of Mount Vernon.

In the mid-nineteenth century, a number of social forces combined to make this house museum movement ideologically desirable, thanks to increased population, immigration, industrialization, class stratification, and tourism. The women who organized themselves into volunteer clubs to preserve historic homes came from established families. Their motives were complex. They wanted to participate in a newfound interest in commemorating the nation's history. They were also invested in enshrining "model homes" that would celebrate domesticity. Preservation and the rise of domestic science went hand in hand. Finally, these women sought to uplift the less fortunate by showing them the proper way to run a household.

In the 1870s and 1880s, historical societies more than doubled in number, and were often based in historic houses. By the 1890s, two house museums a year were being established. In 1890, the Daughters of the American Revolution was founded so that women could "help commemorate the names of the sires of the Revolution." The DAR had an assimilationist ideal. It wanted to Americanize immigrants by inculcating patriotism in them, and they wanted to ensure that historic buildings were safeguarded. In their mission statement they stated their aim to "teach patriotism by erecting monuments and protecting historical spots, by promoting the cause of education, especially the study of history, the enlightenment of the foreign population, and all that makes for good citizenship."

Concord was, of course, a historic place before it was a literary hotbed, and so it was home to some of the nation's first efforts at historic preservation. By 1902 "genuine Thoreau pencils" were sold alongside "Minutemen Stick Pins." Concord's Women's Club was founded in 1895 for "educational and social culture." Membership was selective, and their motto was "Leave the Chaff and Take the Wheat." They held classes, and helping immigrants Americanize was a main theme.

In 1900, Harriet Lothrop, then living in the Alcotts' Wayside home and the author of the *Five Little Peppers* series (which has an uncanny similarity to the *Little Women* books, and was published under her pseudonym Margaret Sidney), bought Orchard House and then sought another buyer who would renovate the falling-down house into a museum in honor of Alcott. She tried to find someone but there were no takers. In 1901, she proposed a fundraising scheme—the Little Women Clubs of America should initiate a one-dollar fee for the first year of membership, and a quarter for every year afterward, to care for Orchard House. Newspapers began covering the decaying house and efforts to preserve it. The *Boston Herald* published a letter from "An Englishwoman" asking, "Why in the name of almost everything that good Americans hold dear should that home of Louisa May Alcott not be bought by public subscription and be made a museum and show place like Washington's home?" Women's clubs and magazines carried on the fundraising: "If all who have in the last fifty years enjoyed the books written in that house, the characters built there, would contribute a small sum the object would be accomplished." The founders saw Orchard House as one of the nation's most beloved houses, an "emblem of the virtuous and ostentatiously traditional domesticity that could establish a reassuring stability as they entered the new world of the twentieth century." They also appealed to the veracity of the house, as it were, stating that the house would provide "conclusive and definitive proof that, after all, the story was true, and not made up out of the author's head."

By the 1910s, the women's rights movement was gaining steam, and the historic house movement's desire to sanctify houses was critiqued by feminists such as Gilman, who believed the focus on the house oppressed women. Some pushed to have Orchard House represent Alcott's feminist views. In 1911, the National American Woman Suffrage Association wrote a letter to the Concord paper stating that, because the house would be open as a memorial in a few months, they might want to "have occasional glimpses of Miss Alcott's views on Woman Suffrage." But the town was then split on suffragism. One founder of Orchard House, Bessie Hudson, became president of the Concord branch of the Massachusetts Association Opposed to the Further Extension of Suffrage to Women. Other founders were pro-suffragists who invoked Louisa May Alcott to prove the worthiness of their cause. Eventually, the founders of the Orchard House museum finessed the question of suffragism when they officially opened, stating that they did not believe in suffrage but believed it to be inevitable, and thus women must prepare for its eventuality. But when, in May 1912, the house opened to the public, it became known as a *Little Women* shrine. Fiction had won out. The intense poverty of the Alcotts, Bronson's radical ideals, Louisa's advocacy for suffrage and unmarried women's function in society and her many lonely years spent laboring in the home to support her parents, were jettisoned in favor of a sentimental view of a typical nineteenth-century home.

Orchard House was one of the first American writers' houses to be preserved as a museum, and one of the first historic sites dedicated to a woman. It is certainly the first woman writer's house museum. However, today, one of the greatest struggles of Orchard House, when asking for funding, is that organizations consider the house a *Little Women* pilgrimage site, and not a historic or educational site.

When you walk into the house today, the first thing you see is a Madame Alexander doll of Louisa May Alcott in a Scarlett O'Hara-esque dress on sale for $125. In this gift-shop lobby, you can buy t-shirts, books, reproductions of nineteenth-century toys, the standard writers' house display.

Admission costs nine dollars, and next to the register is a donation box asking to help fund renovations.

My guide was Betsy, a sweet, fifty-something woman who was a bit nervous as we began our visit in the kitchen. On the tour with me was a woman who grew up in Concord, and had first visited Orchard House with her Brownie troop. She was now on a visit home to take her son and daughter for their first tours. Also in the group were three middle-aged tourists with Australian-sounding accents. One of them was a man, and he often looked under the furniture to see how the joints were constructed.

The line between fact and fiction was continually elided. *Little Women*, it would seem from Betsy's tour, was a memoir. She told us that Louisa "gave herself a boyish name, Jo." When we entered the parlor, she told us that the book described "just exactly as it happened here in 1860, when Meg, or Anna, had her wedding to John."

In May's room, we saw the flowers she painted—still bright—and we spent a long time learning about May's painting career in Europe while standing, cramped and hot, in the small, second-floor bedroom, which had a plaque outside announcing that a grant from the Lowe's Home Improvement Stores was aiding the May Alcott room restoration. In Louisa's room, as we all stared at the tiny desk with the ubiquitous faux manuscript pages on it, Betsy told us that the author taught herself to write right-handed so she could use both hands and keep writing for thirteen hours a day. One of the Australian women asked about a needlepoint linen on the bedside trunk with LMA embroidered on it: "Did she actually do this?" she asks as we file out of the room.

Not all tours are like the one I had with Betsy. Erin Durham, another tour guide, told me guides are trained by shadowing several more experienced tour guides. They are not provided with a written script, but there is a guides' book with suggested information to relay, and a library with extensive resources that guides are encouraged to read. Guides devise their own tours, and alter them for each group.

"You have to tell stories," Durham told me. "And you have to get people engaged. But you need to tailor your tour to who is on it at any given time, whether they are children, or scholars, or students. Some people are here for their pilgrimage. They've waited their whole life to see the house that inspired their favorite book. With them, you have to bring in pieces of *Little Women*. Once, a woman stopped at the mirror and asked in awe, 'Is this the mirror they would have looked in each morning?' Others are interested in May Alcott's painting, so you need to talk about that. Often older couples interested in Transcendentalism take the tour, so they are interested in Bronson. Lots of women college students take the tour too, and mothers bring their daughters. The ideal tour is one where you pick up on who is in the group and tell stories they want to hear."

The funny thing is that almost none of the many who visit Orchard House go down the road just a few houses to the Wayside. Outside of it is a faded sign, under cloudy Plexiglas, that lists "10 Reasons To Visit Wayside." The Wayside, also a former house of the Alcotts, has to resort to desperate measures to induce people to show up. It isn't even listed on the walking map of historic sites they give out at the Colonial Inn.

I walked along the highway to the Wayside, leaving behind the busy Orchard House. The Wayside didn't open until eleven, and I was there earlier than that, so I wandered about for a while, feeling exposed on the Lexington highway. When it opened, a park ranger in his brown uniform was eager to greet me. The admission price to the Wayside is five dollars. The price is subsidized by the federal government, which owns this house, the first national literary monument in the nation.

Wayside, as the sign tells us, was the home to "four writers!" Alcott is one. Nathaniel Hawthorne is another. Harriet Lothrop was its last.

In the visitor center—a barn next to the house—are figures of Hawthorne, standing up at his writing table, and Harriet Lothrop in a rocking chair wearing a shawl. Her hair is in a bun and she has on a lace blouse. On her lap is a sign: "Please Do Not Touch Figures."

In her statue, Louisa is dressed for one of the plays in which Jo performs in *Little Women*. She wears pants and a hat, and is holding a sword. The text on the wall behind states that, "Mothers and daughters all over the world have found that *Little Women* captures most realistically their closest relationships."

Hawthorne moved in after the Alcotts moved out. Louisa lived here as a child, and many of the autobiographical elements of *Little Women*— putting on the pirate play, for instance—happened in this house. But that is not why it is a National Historic Park site. Rather, it is so because Minutemen lived here during the Revolutionary War. John Winthrop lived here, too, in 1775. When Nathaniel Hawthorne died, a cult of celebrity grew up around him (to be supplanted by that of Thoreau and Alcott), and Lothrop wanted to buy the house to preserve it in his honor. The house was built in 1687, and it was in terrible shape when Lothrop acquired it in the 1880s.

It needs work today, too, but when your landlord is the federal government, it can be hard to maintain a house. My guide, Daniel Harrigan, told us that someone once cleaned out the gutters himself and was reprimanded. There's $800,000 coming in an appropriation from Congress, but everyone has to wait before they can make repairs. "It may be a few years, but I can't say why," Harrigan told us, mindful of my notebook. "If there was any way I could have taken care of this place myself I would have done so by now."

The amazing thing about the Wayside is that the Lothrops made it into a writers' house museum themselves. "They kept changes to a minimum to preserve it as a landmark to Hawthorne," Harrigan explained. "They bought it and decided to keep it exactly as they found it. They sacrificed to modernity only the kitchen, which would have been a woodshed. They were ahead of their time in their approach to historic preservation."

The National Park Service preserves the Lothrops' first preservation efforts. All around the house you can still see the signs the Lothrops hung. One reads: "The Old Room. This is the oldest part of the house. . . . The kettle is a Hawthorne kettle." In the library the sign reads: "Here Hawthorne read all of Scott's novels aloud to his children. Mrs. Hawthorne sat at the centre table with her workbasket and the children grouped around. He used this room a great deal for study, during the last years of his life."

The top floor of the house is called the Sky Parlor. You walk up a very narrow set of stairs to enter. Up there are murals that were painted after Hawthorne's death in 1864. There are busts, too, that were originally housed in the Concord School of Philosophy. They should be in Orchard House, or behind it in the restored schoolhouse. But they cannot return them, because that would set a precedent for deaccession. It's tough, Harrigan says, to follow all the rules of the Fed, but it's better than other alternatives, such as: "The Wayside, brought to you by Nokia."

In the Sky Parlor is the standard writers' house fake manuscript on top of the standing desk that Hawthorne used. When you descend the stairs, you pass a cupboard built into the wall on the narrow landing. It was locked for years. Hawthorne's daughter, Rose, opened it after his death. Inside were fragments of novels. Hawthorne used to put his manuscript pages into the cupboard, and then lock it, when he was done writing for the day.

According to a wildly unscientific poll I conducted, most men have not read *Little Women*, which might be why I never read it when I was younger. I was a tomboy, and considered myself a serious reader. Why waste my time on a prissy book for girly girls? Going to Orchard House forced me to read *Little Women*, and I loved every page, and was surprised by its nuance and complexity. Reading about Alcott's life, I was angry I had known so little of it before, annoyed by the myth-making surrounding her that precluded us from seeing her as a Great Man, in Emersonian terms.

Because Orchard House was made into a shrine to the author of a children's book, those who visit it do not gain the kind of cultural capital that those who visit Walden Pond do. Thoreauvian pilgrims are a serious lot, upholding great American ideals. A trip to pay homage at Orchard House will not impress the literati. And since Alcott's reputation as a suffragist, reformer, and activist for women's rights has been forgotten, some women—me, before I learned about Alcott and finally read *Little Women*—might be embarrassed to visit this house.

Erin Durham tells me not many men take the tour, either. "Guys are often sheepish-looking when they start the tour, and you can tell lots of wives drag their husbands," she says. "One of the guides thinks the whole point of these tours is to get a man to like it: that's the goal."

Most of the staff and tour guides are women. "I think Alcott's is a success story that comes at a great price," Durham says. "People don't see the sacrifices entailed to live according to her ideas. I think we should tell the story with the pain involved. The toll it took."

Some of the staff works to do this, but they also need to accommodate the constant demand for sentimental March family stories, the questions about the wedding held in the living room and whether Louisa did her own embroidery.

I ask Durham about Louisa's decision to marry off Jo. "I think it's a shame, because she did want to advocate for unmarried women. But she was very lonely. She had a hard life at the end. I wish for her the *Little Women* ending."

Here's what I wish for Alcott, today: Her books assigned in schools as often as are *Huck Finn* or *Catcher in the Rye*; her reputation remade into that of the tortured romantic genius; it would also be nice to have a foundation in her honor dedicated to offering women writers grants or scholarships for female writers. Let us revere her! If we restore another place in her honor, let it be a place that has no sentimental domestic touches whatsoever—her garrett in Boston, maybe—where she fled whenever she felt her parents could be spared her, away from oppressive Concord and the throngs of March family admirers.

Hemingway's things, Ketchum

Chapter 5

Hemingway's Breadcrumb Trail

> All stories, if continued far enough, end in death, and he
> is no true-story teller who would keep that from you.
> —Ernest Hemingway, *Death in the Afternoon*

I LIKED HEMINGWAY in high school. I had a crush on Jake Barnes, and while affecting a certain world-weariness during my senior year, I would respond to hopes for the world or boyfriends with "Wouldn't it be pretty to think so?"

But by the time I declared an English major in 1985, I had been well trained to hate him. Back then, there was one word for Hemingway— misogynist—and we bandied it about with relish in class discussions. When discussing other writers, we would use his name to shorthand problematic depictions of women: "Hemingwayesque" would put, say, Philip Roth or Seamus Heaney in their places.

Not only among impassioned undergrads (nineteen is, I think, the *ne plus ultra* age for exhortations of misogyny), but also among scholars, Hemingway was on the outs in the 1980s. I do not remember being assigned his novels in class; more experimental modernists like Gertrude Stein, James Joyce, and William Faulkner graced my syllabi. The scholars I read did not cite him much. If there were a word cloud of my experience of American literature then, Hemingway would have been in a very small, angry font.

But Hemingway is a big word—maybe even the biggest word of them all—in the "American literature," "read," and "liked" word cloud. Men who read histories—not novels—often include Hemingway as a favorite, making him the exception to prove their rule. A friend of mine tells me this story at lunch: her twenty-year-old stepson has never been much of a student or a reader. But he started reading novels when he roomed with some scholarly women. He started with Charles Bukowski and loved him. They suggested Chuck Palahniuk, whom he also loved. Then my friend took him to the local used bookstore and asked the owner for more suggestions. She thought he might like Hemingway, so he bought, read, and loved *The Sun Also Rises*. He went back for *A Farewell to Arms, The Snows of Kilimanjaro,* and short stories. Now he has decided to reenroll in community college, and devoured the entire Introduction to Literature reading list before the first day.

I reread Hemingway a few years ago, when I realized I knew more about what others said about Hemingway than I knew about Hemingway himself. Second time around, I still find Jake crush-worthy, *A Farewell to Arms* engrossing, and I can take his sexism with a historical grain of salt.

Hemingway's life has always been as well known as his work—his hard-living ways, his war reporting, his African hunting, and his womanizing. But this famous life story entails selective forgetting. I knew he fought in the Spanish Civil War, but I did not know Fidel Castro was a fan. I knew he was unstable, but I did not know he was institutionalized. Usually, suicide colors a writer's reputation, but Hemingway seems to have escaped being defined by how he ended his life.

Hemingway lived for decades as an American celebrity, and he had an intensely conflicted relationship to publicity. "It is queer to find one's own day before yesterday turning up as literary history," Hemingway wrote to a former professor in a letter.

To Malcolm Cowley he wrote that, "we suffer in our times from an exaggerated emphasis on personality, and I would much rather have my work discussed than the offence of my life." "He hated the idea of the 'shit' that would be written about him and his work after he was dead," Ivan Kashkin wrote.

"It was bad for a writer," Hemingway maintained, "when he started to think of himself as a character." After the infamous Lillian Ross profile of him, he stated that, "He hated . . . having his personal life presented as a subject of study for college students."

Those comments tell only half the story. After all, he publicly made these statements to journalists and critics, who he knew would publish them. At his estate in Cuba, he had a "No Visitor" sign outside his door, but there are dozens and dozens of published interviews with Hemingway that took place *inside*. He said he could not stand thinking about the crappy biographies that would be published after his death, and after Arthur Mizener's controversial F. Scott Fitzgerald biography was published in 1951, he grumped, "Imagine what they can do with the soiled sheets of four legal beds by the same writer and you can see why their tongues are slavering. . . . Every young English professor sees gold in them dirty sheets now." But he told Carlos Baker, who asked for more personal details of his life, that there were some stories he did not want told: "the suicide of my father. This is the best story I never wrote. Then comes Pauline moving in on Hadley; which I would never write." and he continued, telling Baker all the other stories he also did not want told.

Hemingway has always been tabloid fodder and a polarizing figure ("Misogynist!" I hear my younger self saying). There are four preserved Hemingway houses, and local and global controversies surround these houses just as they did Hemingway when he was alive. The controversies over his houses make obvious what is true of all writers' house museums: they are not timeless gems tucked away from the hustle and bustle of the world. They are complicated and complicating parts of the landscape of the present.

Let us start at the end.

On the morning of July 2, 1961, Hemingway woke up in his house in

Ketchum, Idaho. He had just been released from psychiatric care. A few months earlier, his fourth wife, Mary, had found him holding a gun and a note. He was sure the FBI was stalking his rural Idaho home, and was keeping meticulous logs of every minute of his day. He had attempted suicide before. Earlier that year, he had sprinted out of a car and inside his house with the intention to kill himself. Friends ran after him to stop him. But on July 2, he found the keys to the locked storeroom that housed his guns, went back upstairs to his foyer, and shot himself through the mouth.

The Nature Conservancy of America now owns that foyer. I stood in it on a chilly March day, forty-six years after Hemingway's death. I was alone. A wall of plate-glass windows looked out at an expanse of unpeopled, dormant mountains, trees, and valleys. The room has been preserved: the same furniture, bookshelves, rugs, and wall furnishings that Hemingway looked at the day he killed himself remain in place. The room looks nothing like one expects Hemingway to be comfortable in, with its mid-century suburban sleek lines, fluffy white chair, and pink and green patterned couch. Jarringly, an opened, half-empty box of bullets sits on the bookshelf, a morbid version of the "author will be right back" displays of dishes and clothes we find in other houses.

The house is not open to the public. It is managed by Taylor Paslay, whose main job is to decide who does and does not go inside. Lots of people try to sneak in, and he runs them off. But if you are a scholar or have a legitimate reason to see the house, Paslay will allow you to do so. Paslay respects all requests from readers, mostly Europeans. He is happy to accommodate their desire to see Hemingway's house, but does not understand their urge. "I am a huge music fan, but I never wanted to see Hendrix's grave, even when I lived in Seattle," he told me. He is trying to figure out the demographic of people who want to see the house. "Hunters," he tells me. "They are mainly hunters of some sort."

I flew to Ketchum after Paslay gave me permission to visit, and once I got there he left me to wander about on my own. I stood very still, and felt a slight vertigo at one point that I could only attribute to altitude—or anxiety. What is one supposed to feel while in such a place? My notebook in my hand seemed a rude affront. Should one jot down notes while standing in such a space? What questions was I supposed to ask?

The Ketchum house was not the first Hemingway house I had been to. In January, I had spent a few sunnier days in Key West, Florida, and toured his much noisier house.

The Hemingway House and Museum is the only private, for-profit writer's house museum in the country. It is also the most visited. It draws enormous crowds—cruise ship passengers on day trips line up all the way down the block, waiting to pay their admission. The website, hemingwayhome.com, has live 24/7 streaming.

There is a third world feel to this southernmost town of the continental United States. It is funky, but chain-store ridden at the same time. It still has a sense of place—a sort of bohunk tropical torpor and lassitude. The guy on the street wearing the straw stovepipe hat and holding a hand painted "dirty jokes: $1.00" sign is really that drunk, and slightly falling off his chair. He is a lecherous drunk, a hard-living fish-tale character. He is ogled by French and German tourists in crisp pastel tank tops, chunky gold jewelry, and too-tight white shorts who are happy to be surrounded by local color.

When I stopped for a before-dinner drink at Awful Arthur's, the kind of place that wants to be a "real" Key West bar—but is really just a sports bar that serves oysters—the guy who was sitting next to me (replete with a Hawaiian shirt and a cell phone clipped to his belt) was slurring his words into nonsense; his buddy, sporting a naughty cupid tattoo, was chatting up the woman next to him. I felt warm and fuzzy amidst the decrepitude of the place.

The airport cab driver had told me that in five years, the Hemingway House would be ruined, because the place is not taken care of and lacks air conditioning. It contains few actual Hemingway possessions. Like Key West, the Hemingway house is sincerely fake. It is the inside out, obverse of Hannibal. This place is out to make a buck, and does not pretend to be doing anything but. Therein lies its charm.

When I arrived at the Key West house, an Asian couple stopped me and, through gestures, asked if I could take a picture of them next to the "Hemingway House" sign. The man sitting in the ticket booth was a dead ringer for Truman Capote, and he charged me eleven dollars to get in. A plaque on the house told me this has been a National Historic Landmark since 1968; a sign on the front walk gave me the web site for the house.

Not quite ready for the serious work of note taking and interviewing, I decided to go to the gift shop first. In front were two Penny Pincher souvenir coin machines. They must date from the early 1960s, when the place first opened. The gears and cranks were rusting. There were handwritten signs that told me how to make my penny into a souvenir. If I did it wrong, there would be no refunds, the signs warned. I read the signs carefully, turned the huge crank four times. The penny came out thin and oblong, as it should, but with nothing stamped on it.

On the gift shop door were more handwritten signs: "Trivia Question of the Day: How old was Ernest Hemingway When He was Born? And "Welcome to the Bookstore: All the Hemingway With Only Half the Fat."

The gift shop was somnolent. The paint was peeling in huge gashes; it had been peeling for decades, and the place smelled like sawdust. Handmade bookshelves lined the small cramped rooms. They were having a clearance sale on the photos of Hemingway, indicated by red dots on the top of the prints. They were all old black and white publicity shots, tacked up one next to the other in an apparent rush, squeezed for space in the tiny room. They'd been there a long time, red dots and all; the edges were curled forward, the images faded.

On the display shelves below, there were cat etchings, address books, paperweights, catnip in little bottles, magnets, and key chains. All books sold here, a sign tells us, "are embossed with the seal of the Hemingway house."

For $25.49 you could buy a Hemingway home collector's plate made in England and etched with a blue porcelain picture of the house. On the back of the plate, there's an image of a scroll listing the books that Hemingway wrote while at the house. There was also a hand-made poster for sale— "The Hemingway Women!"—that contains black and white photographs of the author's great loves, arranged chronologically from left to right. Under Agnes von Kurowsky's image, a handwritten caption reads: "She Said No Thanks!"

There was a floating cap pen, a Christmas tree ornament ball with a picture of the house on it, tiles with cat faces painted on them, Hemingway cookies ("Key Lime Cookies!"), placemats, hats, pencils, an autograph by Mariel Hemingway surrounded by four studio shots of her in matted peek-a-boo frames ($115), shot glasses, a book of cat poems, and thirteen different kinds of t-shirts, including one that depicted a cat sitting by a typewriter on the porch.

I left the gift shop with a Hemingway House and Museum snow globe (replete with cats lounging in front of the house, and confetti instead of snow). I then headed to the porch where the tour guides were sitting on benches, heads down between splayed legs, smoking, and obviously hungover. I took a seat next to them, feeling a bit obvious and nervous. All of them were wizened middle-aged men wearing Hawaiian shirts and fisherman's caps and facial hair. They didn't pay me much mind.

I listened as they exchanged stories about places in town that will clean your shrimp—de-vein them, too. "Publix got a good thing going over there," says Greg—whose name I knew because he sports a nametag that also indicates his home state of New Jersey. Greg and his coworkers all had southern accents, though none of them were Floridian or even remotely southern.

I gathered my courage and asked if I could ask them some questions. Why, I wanted to know, do they think people come here?

Greg told me that people come to this house because, "they just want to walk where Hemingway walked. But they don't want to hear the bad. New England types get offended by the urinal—you know, where the water for the cats is? I don't know why."

I asked him what people do when they get upset. "They walk off the tour, call the office, and complain. Lots of people wait their whole life to come here. They don't like to hear dirt. They want a little bit of the bad, but not too much. You can see a reverence. The writing studio? You know, up where his typewriter is? That's like Mecca for these people. I've had lots of people, mainly English teachers, who say they'll give me twenty bucks 'if you let me type on the typewriter.'"

The guys told me that during the high season, the house employs six guides, who each average six tours a day. That's thirty-six tours, with an average thirty-five people a tour, 365 days a year. When it is busy, they do tours about five minutes apart. They work "all day long, hard and fast." For training, the guides are given a fact sheet, and an older tour guide gives them a tour. They are not required to read any Hemingway or any biographies.

Tipping is encouraged on the tours, they said, and Loren—whose nametag claimed that his hometown is "The Sea"—and Greg began talking about a former guide who made the most in tips. "He bashed Hemingway the whole time. The facts came out the same, but the angle was different," Loren told me.

There's an egalitarian order for tours, so everyone gets a chance to make as many tips as possible. In his first week, Greg made enough in tips to put a $650 down payment on his scooter.

As we sat talking, the guides played a game, guessing the nationality of people lining up to buy tickets. "What do you think? German or French?" Loren asked Greg of a party at the booth window.

"Well, that woman just walked away when she heard the price of admission," Greg noted.

"German," Loren said. "Definitely German."

Loren worked for thirty-five years as a lineman in Missouri, and his voice had the mellow drawl of the mid-South, only more attenuated since being struck four years ago by the "Keys Disease." "My wife and I came down here for two weeks four years ago," he explained.

Loren was the most Papa-ish of all the guides, with a crisp gray Cuban shirt, harsh blue eyes, and just the right gray scraggly beard. He wore a gold boat steering wheel earring. He was handsome—sinewy, taut—and he knew he could weave a good tale. The other guides considered his the best tour to take, so I joined Loren for the 12:15.

There were about ten other people on the tour with me, and I could not guess why any one of them was there, though I imagined that most were simply visiting Key West and stopped here as part of their day's itinerary.

As we enter the living room, crammed with knick-knacks, bad portraits of elk, sentimental renderings of cats, and faded photocopies of newspaper articles, Loren started his tour by telling us, "If you see a Kodak moment, hop in it."

"All the artwork is local talent or on display, " he continued. He went on to give us the standard docent information about the century and style of this or that chair or table, which was absurd given how terribly this unremarkable house was curated. There was foggy, chipped Plexiglas over the photographs and displays. Still, Loren reminded us not to touch any of it.

Loren carefully timed his punch lines in the Hemingway dining room. He made Pauline, Hemingway's second wife, into the antagonist of his tour. He joked about how Pauline took out the ceiling fan to install pretentious chandeliers, so the house was always insufferably hot. "It would be priceless to me if Pauline would be reincarnated as a summer tour guide for the house," he noted as he led us out of the dining room.

Loren milked his folksy charm. Of a photograph of people fishing off Cuba, he pointed out one man and said that he was probably Joe Kennedy Sr. "I've often wondered . . . Joe Kennedy Senior . . . I wonder what that character would be doing in Cuba during Prohibition," he said, and then patiently waited for our laughs. After he told us about Hemingway's fishing companion Gregorio Fuentes, he took out his flask and toasted him. He told us that Hemingway was "surrounded by an accumulation of ex-wives."

Loren told us Hemingway's years in this house were his "insomniac years," suffering as he did with manic depression, and then showed us the birthing stool in the bedroom. He also told us Hemingway did a majority of his writing while here, writing *A Farewell to Arms* by hand, and getting his "writer's revenge: he kills off characters."

As Loren took us upstairs to Hemingway's bedroom, one fellow tour goer whispered to her friend, "He's very good," and then proceeded to ask Loren how long he'd been working there. "About seven years," he responded. "But I might be leaving soon. I had to wear long pants past twice last week. That's not why I moved down here. Plus, Key West is changing. Shrimp is $4.99 a pound now. All the shrimp boats have left. The only way to live here is to live on a boat. Competition from Vietnamese and the cost of living is killing shrimp men."

After we left the house, we hung out near the pool, which Loren told us was built in 1937 and was the first in-ground pool ever in the Keys. Pauline spent $20,000 on it, and the price prompted Hemingway to take a penny from his pocket and press it into the wet cement of the surrounding patio and yell: "Here, take the last penny I've got!"

Then Loren showed us a penny melted into the ground. Ka-ching.

Loren ended his tour leaning against a wall under a "If you enjoyed your tour, tips are appreciated" sign. The sign was not ratty homespun cute, like so many of others around the place. It was nicely made on sturdy green wood with yellow text, matching the paint tones of the house.

"The house sold to Bernice Dickson in 1961," Loren told us. "She did not like living here, because there were people at the front door all hours to see the house. She left the estate to the tour company. I'm delighted she did. Thank you."

After the tour, I sat and continued to chat with Loren. "Lots of people think I'm Hemingway," he noted. Sometimes, when another guide is giving a tour, he said he sits on the toilet that looks out on the second floor balcony, reading a book. People do double takes, sometimes scream, thinking they have seen a ghost. I asked Loren what he thinks people are looking to find here. "I don't think they know what they're looking for. But they leave here happy," he responds.

I asked if he's a Hemingway fan. He isn't, he said. I asked him if he understands the people who wait their whole lives to visit the house of their favorite writer, and who consider this house a sacred site. "I was that way about Mark Twain," he starts. "I've read just about all of Twain, excepting a few letters I guess. He could stack the truth right in your face and make you laugh. I love the little pieces. There's a chapter in *Roughing It*, 'Lost in the Desert.' Cracks me up every time I read it. I can just visualize all of it. But his best stuff is from the lecture circuit. He and Will Rogers both, they just took on those pointy-headed politicians. I went to his house in Hannibal."

"What were you looking to find?" I asked.

"Hard to figure why I went. I went hoping to learn something I didn't know before."

"Did you find it?"

"Nope. But I had a good weekend in Hannibal."

Loren is an entertainer, and a reader, and he knows that what we want from Hemingway's House and Museum is a good story. The story is not in the provenance of the dining room table or the birthing stool. It's all in the telling.

Meeting Loren stole all the snark from me. He gives us a tour of a ruin—the dilapidated house of an American literary celebrity that's crammed with relics as scandalously fake as those bought by medieval supplicants. He then asks for tips at the end before sending us off to the gift shop to pick up our own pieces of the cross. He does his job in good faith, and he understands both why folks want a Hemingway snow globe and why I, the pointy-headed English professor, want to sit on the porch with him and ask him questions.

After the tour, I asked Loren for a suggestion for lunch. "I like that place right across the street," he said, slightly lowering his voice. "They have cheeseburgers that would put Jimmy Buffett to shame. Tell them Loren sent you. And tell Larry you're coming back after lunch."

I did what Loren told me. Larry, doing his best Truman Capote voice, said, "Ooohhh, you're going there? You must take this coupon. You'll get a free rum punch. They have the best grouper sandwich."

Hemingway left Key West because he was tired of being on display: too many people passed by his Key West house trying to get a peek at him. Plus, he found the place lax: "It's a soft life," he said of Key West. "Nothing's really happening to me here and I've got to get out." Tired of his Florida digs, he purchased new homes in both Idaho and Cuba.

Hemingway initially went to Sun Valley, the area that encompasses Ketchum, to help promote the place. In the 1930s and 1940s, Sun Valley was a celebrity retreat, like Telluride or Aspen are today. The president of Union Pacific and former New York governor, Averill Harriman, built Sun Valley. Harriman wanted to create a winter resort for passengers on the train from the East Coast to the West. To entice tourists, he paid for movie stars to come out and stay at his glitzy resort, the Sun Valley Lodge. Gary Cooper and Clark Gable were frequent guests during the snow season.

But the warmer months were still slow, so Harriman brought in celebrities to amp up the place's potential as a summer hideaway as well. Hemingway first came to Ketchum in 1939, a few weeks after Hitler invaded Poland. Harriman invited him back for the summer of 1940. The Sun Valley Lodge footed the bill so that, as Hemingway wrote, "the railroad could tell the literature world that we were there, and could take a reasonable number of pictures of the Hemingways at play. In return for this everything was on the house." Hemingway wrote part of *For Whom the Bell Tolls* in a room at the lodge.

Also in 1939, Hemingway and his second wife, Pauline, purchased Finca Vigia, an estate outside Havana, Cuba. They were local celebrities, and entertained many visitors. Cuba was Hemingway's home for twenty years. During this time, he divorced Pauline, married Martha Gellhorn, divorced her, and then married Mary Welsh. He wrote *The Old Man and the Sea* as well as *A Moveable Feast* and *Islands in the Stream,* both published posthumously.

It became difficult for the Hemingways to remain in Cuba by the late 1950s. Batista and Castro's forces were fighting, and people were being tortured and killed near the Hemingway estate. At one point, Hemingway and Mary loaded their boat, the *Pilar,* with ammunition, hoping to help the counterinsurgency. When things got worse, they took the *Pilar* out to sea and dumped the cache. In the meantime, Hemingway was receiving flak in the States for residing in Cuba. Some reported he was siding with Castro. *Esquire* reprinted some of his Spanish Civil War articles—specifically those in which he wrote about fighting alongside Russians. Hemingway's mental health began to plummet and his paranoia escalated. He began to keep obsessive daily notes on his weight, his taxes, and his suspicions that the FBI was following him.

He decided to leave Cuba for a while and go to Ketchum in the fall of 1957. No longer the playboy, Hemingway kept to himself. He did not have drinks in the bar at the Sun Valley Lodge, but instead stayed home or went out with locals, mostly hunting and fishing buddies from twenty years before. With them, there was "almost no literary talk, for most of his hunter friends were not bent that way, saying right out that they had never read any of Ernest's work."

Ernest and Mary returned to Cuba that spring; but before they did, they agreed that, when they returned to the United States, they would move to Ketchum permanently. They found a house on seventeen acres atop the Big Wood River, a forbidding, fortress-like house made of gray concrete. They paid $50,000 in cash for it.

The next fall they returned to their new home in Ketchum. Buick paid the couple to drive there all the way from Key West in the company's new Roadmaster convertible for a commercial. They arrived in November, their relationship in an even greater state of disrepair than the year before. Ernest and Mary notoriously wrote each other nasty letters while living under the same roof. Still, they continued to travel extensively—to New York, Europe, and Cuba, and back to Ketchum. But things only got worse. Hemingway's mental state continued to deteriorate. He was institutionalized several times over the next few years.

In 1959, Castro threatened to appropriate all American property. Hemingway became distraught over the thought of never returning to Cuba again. Then, in 1961, just a few days before the Bay of Pigs, Hemingway tried to kill himself. Right around the Cuban missile crisis, he tried again. This time he succeeded.

Shortly after her husband's death, Mary received a phone call from Castro's minister of foreign affairs. They wanted the Finca Vigía to make it into a memorial to Hemingway. Mary refused. They did it anyway.

When Hunter S. Thompson, a Hemingway fan, learned that Hemingway was living in Ketchum when he took his life, he jumped into his car and drove to Idaho. "When news of his death made headlines in 1961 there must have been other people besides myself who were not as surprised by the suicide by the fact that the story was date-lined Ketchum, Idaho," Thompson wrote in a *Rolling Stone* article called "What Lured Hemingway to Ketchum?"

"What was he doing living there? When had he left Cuba?" Thompson asked. "Anybody who considers himself a writer or even a serious reader cannot help but wonder just what it was about this outback little Idaho village that struck such a responsive chord in America's most famous writer."

Thompson grew to like the area and the shadow of Hemingway that fell over it. He returned often, and on one visit he stole a pair of elk horns that hung over the entrance to the Hemingway's house. He was thrilled to confiscate the horns: "Forget running with the bulls or reeling in marlins or slaughtering rhinos. I had Hemingway's horns, and with that came an immense literary responsibility. It was now 'Fuck you' to the competition. I had broken from the pack, and there was no turning back."

In 2005, Thompson took his own life. As Hemingway had, he shot himself inside his rural western home.

In the 1960s, the Nature Conservancy had little presence in Idaho. But when Mary died in 1986, she left the house and surrounding property to the wildlife preservation organization. She wanted the house to become a nature library and the land, a reserve. She explicitly stated she did not want it made into a museum. She wanted to avoid another "Key West disaster."

The house was built by Bob Topping in the 1950s. His brother, Dan, owned the New York Yankees and was married to Lana Turner. Topping was well known in Ketchum, and rumor has it that he was no longer welcome at the Sun Valley Lodge given his hard-partying ways, so he built the house for private parties. It is Ketchum's "first fourth house," as Paslay, the house's curator, puts it—historic in its own right. "It was extravagant for the time, as fancy as the lodge. Crazy for a former mining town. It was a party palace."

Topping modeled the house after the lodge. It has the same eaves and the same concrete walls. The inside is lined with faux wood paneling. But it is furnished in pure early 1960s, suburban-style, mid-century décor.

At first, the Nature Conservancy simply used the house as its central office. At some point, in the early 1990s, a group of Hemingway fans created the Idaho Hemingway House Foundation, aimed to preserve the Hemingway history of the house. The IHHF put some belongings that remained inside, such as books, under Plexiglas. It was indiscriminate about preserving what it found, so a copy of E. L. Doctorow's *Ragtime*, published in 1975, sits besides copies of books Hemingway may have owned. The group also made displays out of some photos of Hemingway and his friends—and is responsible for setting out those morbid, leftover bullets.

Other Hemingway items were displayed, too: a trunk stamped with the symbol of the Finca Vigia, some pairs of boots, snowshoes, and a Coca Cola cooler from 1950s Cuba. Through these items, the Cuba and Ketchum houses are bound together, since all the possessions were brought to Idaho from the Finca Vigia. Even the desk was shipped from Cuba.

The Nature Conservancy did not ask Mary for the house: it was willed to them. Historic homes are not their bailiwick. It has kept the house as it always was: the lime green molding and Brady Bunch-like living room are all still intact. Mary left some money for upkeep, but it no longer covers costs. The house runs at a loss. In 2003, the IHHF came up with a plan to open the house to the public. It hoped the home would create a new tourist destination in town and bring in money to assist with its upkeep. The group developed a plan to eventually buy the house from the Conservancy, but promised to continue to manage it according to Mary's original mission by preserving the property.

The proposal, however, was stopped by a lawsuit. Three property own-ers—the three neighbors who own houses on the same small road as the Hemingway house—sued the IHHF. They objected to the creation of a museum. Why? Theirs are multimillion-dollar manses, and they did not want *hoi polloi* trespassing over their grounds to gawk. The easy conclusion to leap to is that greedy wealthy folks stopped the museum, and that their private property rights tragically trumped the cause of literature and literary history.

But that conclusion is complicated by the fact that Mary clearly stated that she, too, did not want the Ketchum house to become, like Key West, a tourist trap.

Back in Cuba, Castro had confiscated the house that is today Museu Hem-ingway. What they couldn't bring back to Ketchum, Mary Hemingway was forced to leave behind, including valuable art and reams of papers, manu-scripts, and files Hemingway kept in his isolated tower office. Just after his death, U.S. citizens were prohibited from traveling to Cuba. To this day, Americans who want to view the house can only do so through means of illegal tourism or on some professional tours. I, however, decided not to sneak in the country or take a state-run tour, and so my experience of this house museum has been ironically limited to the written history of it—

adding yet another layer of uncertainty and gray area to the fascinatingly complicated and always political stories of the Hemingway houses.

By the time Mary returned to the Finca Vigia in 1962, the Cuban government had already confiscated the valuables in the safe-deposit boxes the Hemingways kept at the bank. Government surveyors had also been to the estate to inventory possessions, and a painting by Braque was missing. But everything else seemed to be there when Mary looked around. Hemingway was a pack rat, and the place was stuffed with things. Mary's staff was still at the estate, and together they hauled out wheelbarrows full of old magazines and newspapers and burned them in a bonfire. News of her actions quickly leaked to the U.S. Fans were outraged. Glenway Westcott wrote a letter to the *New York Times* protesting Mary's actions. He claimed that she was destroying Hemingway's literary legacy by burning his papers. But she was not.

Instead, Mary was trying to create a diversion, while she quietly put her husband's important papers into boxes and tried to smuggle them out, including thirty to forty pounds of manuscripts. But she did not know how she would get their art collection out of the country, as the Council of Culture prohibited the paintings to be exported. So she invited over Castro himself. Mary describes her plans in her memoir *How It Was*:

> Our doctor, Jose Luis Herrera, an ardent revolutionist and now chief of the medical section of Fidel's army, came out to one of my austerity dinners—there were only a few packages left in the deep freeze—and helped resolve the impasse. He telephoned one of Fidel's aides saying I needed help with a problem. Half an hour later the aide called to say that the Prime Minister would be at the Finca the following afternoon. . . . In a flash of whimsey I opted for giving Fidel the old-fashioned welcome of Spain in which all the household lines up outside the entrance to greet a visitor. I alerted the gardeners. . . . They were all in a place, double row of welcomers, about eight o'clock when the Prime Minister arrived in his jeep, accompanied only by one nondescript car. In the sitting room, he headed for Ernest's chair and was seating himself when I murmured that it was my husband's favorite. The Prime Minister raised himself, up, slightly abashed. "No, no, señor, please be seated there."

Then Mary gave him a tour. Castro seemed impressed as she led him through the house. He commented on his interest in some taxidermy. Mary explained that she couldn't leave the paintings in Cuba, but was struggling to get them back to Ketchum. "Why don't you stay here with us in Cuba?" he asked her.

Mary's plan had worked. Castro offered to help her transport her paintings back to the United States and he promised to leave the guesthouse untouched, "for your use when you may return."

Mary received instructions to have her boxes in a pier in Havana at 8 A.M. the following morning. Tied up at the pier was a shrimp boat from Tampa, one of the last of the fleets that had plied between Cuba and Florida, carrying shrimp and other fish from Cuban waters in refrigerated bottoms back to U.S. markets. It was the last approved ship from the United States.

Before leaving Cuba for the last time, Mary discussed plans for what to do with the *Pilar*, the Hemingways' beloved boat, with his sailing partner Gregorio. "Take all our fishing gear, rods, reels, line, everything, to use yourself or sell or as you wish, before the government claims it," she told him.

As for the boat, she asked him to take the boat out to sea and sink it. He never did.

Hemingway never anticipated it being a Cuban landmark, and Mary daringly took what she could from the house back to the States. She did not want the Finca to be a museum—she did not even want it to become property of the state. It was forcibly confiscated from her. It is now one of the major tourist attractions in Cuba, and the Finca tours, along with the many Hemingway-themed restaurants and bars and items for sale in Cuba, make money for the state. Hemingway never shied from making money off his name, and neither have his progeny. But of all the posthumous fates Hemingway may have imagined for himself, I doubt this one entered into his tortured consciousness. It is, however, suitable, as Hemingway seemed to always get himself enmeshed in political battles, sometimes despite himself. As he aged, he tried to sequester himself from the messy politics of his youth, moving to places where he could get away from it all, like the estate he bought in Cuba.

Today, the town of Ketchum has recovered some of its glory, but it is tough for the locals to survive. As people told me over and over while I was there, the area is once again—as it was in the 1940s—a place for "fourth houses and fourth wives." The first thing everyone says to you when you're in

Ketchum, Idaho, is: "Not easy to get here, is it?" It is not. For me, it meant one scratched attempt—we got stuck in Fort Wayne, Indiana, overnight due to weather, and I went back home. The second time I made it: Cleveland to Salt Lake City to Hailey/Sun Valley, the nearest airport. Since planes are often grounded in Hailey, most people just drive the three hours from Boise. Or they fly themselves. Hailey is the second busiest airport in Idaho, and 80 percent of the jets taking off and landing are privately owned. In the glossy magazine they give out in the hotel, three private aviation firms advertise their services.

Also advertised in Sun Valley is Ernest Hemingway. I stayed at the Sun Valley Lodge, where Hemingway played in the 1940s. I was put in a small room on the first floor. Hemingway always stayed in Room 206 upstairs. Now the room is the Hemingway Suite, the most expensive room in the lodge. The manager gave me a tour: on the walls are photos of Papa laughing with Gary Cooper and, on the dresser, a strangely beautiful bronze statue of Hemingway typing.

Hanging around Ketchum for a few days, I realized most residents and tourists know Hemingway lived there—one man came for a weekend just because of the writer's presence—but no one I talked to knew he had committed suicide here. A taxi driver told me that I was wrong, that he died of disease. Others also did not know he had died in Ketchum, though they knew he lived there.

The Nature Conservancy cannot bring itself to unload the house, although Mary's will put no restrictions on a future sale. Rather, its refusal to do so is "for ethical and legal reasons," Paslay tells me. "It's a local landmark. The most requested question the Chamber of Commerce gets is where is the Hemingway house. It's a moral thing. The price would be so tremendous. Given the local economy and ways of doing things here, the house would be destroyed and a new mansion put up. We have a conservation ethic at the Nature Conservancy. This is the largest undeveloped property in Ketchum. We're in charge of the easement. We have a responsibility for not just house but the land. We made a decision that we would take responsibility and be able to do this for the community." They have changed their pitch: now they focus on the land, and how much Hemingway loved it. It helps them reel in potential donors: they bring them to the house, show them the view. Now they see the house as a loss leader: "the cost of house versus what we get out of it is immeasurable. We take donors here and when they pass they may leave us money."

I talk to several locals who wished the house were a museum, and are resentful of those who protested it. At a bookstore, I talked with a clerk who is a long-time resident. She says the economy is not doing great, partly because it is so hard to get here. There is not much for nonskiers to do, and the downtown is filled with little more than banks. There are many second, third, and fourth home owners who fly in and out, spending maybe two weeks a year here. It's good for the service economy—the housekeepers and landscapers. But those people do not live in town, for the most part: the Sun Valley Lodge spends $15,000 a month on gas to bus their workers 85 miles each way from Twin Falls, where housing is affordable. The staff is mostly European and South American. But for people like the bookstore clerk, it leaves Ketchum without a sense of community. In her subdivision, she's the only full-time resident, so she doesn't have any neighbors. She would welcome the increased tourist activity she imagines would ensue if the Hemingway house were open to the public.

The IHHF foundation disbanded and gave back the money they had raised to the donors. Paslay has since gotten to know the neighbors, and they now get along. They ask him to keep an eye on their places when they are out of town. "The Nature Conservancy believes in being a good neighbor, even to people who aren't conservation friendly," he says.

The Museu Hemingway is one of the biggest tourist attractions in Cuba, where Hemingway, like cigars, is a major draw. Most cannot go inside this Hemingway house either, but busloads of tourists drive by many times a day to see it from the outside, and to see the (never sunk) *Pilar* on the lawn. Suffering from the same tropical torpor and antiquated preservation practices as does the Key West house, it was declared a "Preservation Emergency" by the National Trust in 2002. The Finca Vigia touts itself as "the only living museum of Ernest Hemingway, meaning the home has not changed in the arrangement of its belongings since the author was in residence."

In 2002, Fidel Castro showed up at the Museu Hemingway in San Francisco de Paula, Cuba. The occasion was the signing of an earlier agreement between Cuba and the United States to preserve the Finca Vigia. There to greet him were Hemingway's step-grandson and niece, the granddaughter of Hemingway's editor Max Perkins, the director of the Cuban National Heritage Council, and others. Castro arrived with guards carrying submachine guns. "I think we would be savages if we did not recognize the importance of preserving this place," he proclaimed. "His work *For Whom the Bell Tolls* had a significant influence on my life personally. I had to put into practice an idea in order to face a very complex political situation in our country. We started from scratch, basically; we had no weapons, no guns. We had to solve the situation of how to defeat a regime that had seventy to eighty thousand well-armed and well-equipped men, and a government that had international support and seemed invincible. How could we face that situation when all other legal and constitutional avenues had been closed to this country and its citizens? I remembered the point [in *For Whom the Bell Tolls*] where the entire plot developed. A small patrol of cavalry behind the front line draws near to an area where combat is taking place; a man with a machine gun watches that patrol unity from a distance. In our history there is the story about a feud between the farmers and the landowners who had evicted them from their land. A journalist explained this in such places one man, well placed, could stop an army. I have always kept in my memory Hemingway's description of what happens behind enemy lines. It was an awakening. I have never forgotten that book."

Castro continued to pronounce the moral imperative to preserve history: "What is a man without history? Without history we would not even have an idea of how limited the work of the human species is. The human species continues to make mistakes all the time. Just a few days ago, we had a visit here from a very well known American filmmaker, Mr. Steven Spielberg. He showed his films in a small festival, one of them the very impressive *Schindler's List*, which is a very well known film in our country. Seeing how great historical monuments are destroyed—the big statues, the Buddhas that were destroyed in Afghanistan—I wonder whether mankind has really reached any degree of civilization. . . . You wonder, are we really civilized?"

When Castro met Hemingway in 1960, he caught the biggest fish in Hemingway's marlin tournament. Hemingway presented Castro with the winner's cup. A picture was taken: two famous beards smiling at each other. Castro keeps that picture in his office. However, it is illegal to sell Hemingway's books on the island, as they contain content deemed unfit for Cuba's citizens.

Castro calling those who do not honor the past savage and uncivilized is ironic at best—he makes money off the place and allows it to fall into disrepair. When the house was declared a "preservation emergency" he jumped on the chance for a photo op; President George W. Bush, meanwhile, opposed any American dollars spent to preserve it.

And what would Hemingway have wanted to happen to these houses? This question arises for every author with a house museum, of course. What would he or she think of us tromping through this house, snooping around his or her stuff? Hemingway became very famous very young, and lived for decades as a celebrity writer and a figure in American culture. He knew he would have a posthumous life. He both desired this attention and fiercely guarded against the very prospect. His suicide makes the question all the more complex, since he chose the moment of his demise. Did he leave us directions for how to dispose of his literary estate or his intellectual and personal property? If he did, are we obligated to follow them?

We know so much about Hemingway's life—that Pauline took out the fans to put in chandeliers at Key West, and that his father killed himself—because Hemingway preserved every last scrap of his life. His biographer James Mellow suspects that he "deliberately salvaged his diaries, papers, letters, and the many drafts of his stories and novels, transporting them across oceans and from residence to residence, for the express purpose of making them available for scholarly study," and that "he seems to have anticipated, even collaborated in it to the extent of saving the necessary documentary material for such a life: all the various notebooks, diaries, passports, correspondence."

Six years after Castro's speech on the lawn of the Finca, not much more has been done to the house. American money cannot be spent for restoration, and Castro siphoned some funds for repair of hurricane damage in 2008. When Valerie Hemingway visited in 2007, she said Hemingway was "everywhere." "The Hemingway I encountered on my ten-day visit was both more benign and more Cuban than that one I knew. . . . There seems almost a proprietary interest in him, as if, with the yawning gap between the U.S. and Cuba, the appropriation of the American author gave his adopted country both solace and a sense of one-upmanship."

Conspiratorially, curators whisper to visiting non-American journalists that it will be Europeans that finally send the Finca the funds it needs.

Which is it? Are we savages if we do not preserve the Museu Hemingway or is the act of preserving the Finca Vigía, full of items forcibly confiscated by Castro, savage? Are those who prohibited Hemingway's Ketchum house from becoming a museum savages, or is it a savage act to preserve the living room to the exact moment of despair? Is Key West a horrid tourist trap, the guides uncivilized? Or are Loren and his fellow guides the ones who understand best the allure of the house, and who provide thousands with a memorable experience?

Hemingway knew where everything was when he picked up that rifle in 1961. We just keep following his breadcrumb trail. But if the crumbs remain, the ground below them shifts: it goes into government hands, becomes exclusive private property, is leased out for an easy buck. The Hemingway houses with their controversies—kitschy entertainment, economic inequality, corrupt politics—are as representative of our time as Hemingway's writings are of his.

On the way back to the airport from the Sun Valley Lodge, I shared a ride with a couple from Kansas. The man was an oral surgeon who has read all of Hemingway's novels and the author was "half the reason" they came to Sun Valley, though they did not realize he had died in Ketchum, and insisted to me that he had died of cancer, not suicide. Like his literary idol, the surgeon has been to Africa to hunt. Next year, he is going to Key West with a buddy. They plan to go to Sloppy Joe's, and the house, and do "all that Hemingway stuff."

The Old Kentucky Home,
Asheville, North Carolina

Chapter 6

Not That Tom Wolfe

THE THOMAS WOLFE MEMORIAL, in downtown Asheville, North Carolina, is being swallowed up. New developments are dwarfing the yellow frame house on every side, like that little pink house in Virginia Lee Burton's classic children's book. First, the Renaissance Hotel went up across the street. Then, in the summer of 2006, a developer scooped up a parking lot catty-corner from the Renaissance and began construction on upscale condominiums.

As I sat on the rocking chair on the porch of the Memorial on a spring day, I watched workers across the street fill in the outlines of a bathroom in a building that would soon house the young professionals and retirees now choosing to live (or live out their days) in Asheville.

I suppose it is fitting that hotel rooms and condos are engulfing the Memorial, which was originally a boardinghouse run by Julia Wolfe, Tom's mother. The house was formerly called "The Old Kentucky Home," and was never a domestic, single-family residence. It was a business and housed guests from one night to one month. As Hanna Raskin, a former docent, put it, "This isn't a writer's house. It's a historical commercial site."

Though rambling and large, the Memorial on Market Street, a busy central Asheville thoroughfare, is becoming increasingly harder to find. So too is the man to whom the house is dedicated. Thomas Wolfe is fading from view. Go to your local Borders and try to find a copy of his best-known novels: *Look Homeward, Angel* or *You Can't Go Home Again.* You will likely strike out. Scan college syllabi for American literature courses. You will find few weeks, if any, devoted to Wolfe. I have a Ph.D. in English and I was never assigned Wolfe in college or graduate school; no one even suggested I read him for my field exams on American literature.

Yet, Wolfe was once a literary lion, famous for his prose and infamous for his hard-drinking, bad-boy behavior. His death from tuberculosis at the relatively young age of thirty-seven (eighteen days before his thirty-eighth birthday) only added to his mystique in the mid-twentieth century. When I told my seventy-something mother that I was going to the Thomas Wolfe house, she immediately started talking about Aline Bernstein, the older woman with whom Wolfe had a long affair. "It was a big thing when I was a girl," she recalled. "Everyone read him and talked about him and his life." A generation later, though, his reputation had plummeted. A well-read, forty-something friend of mine thought "You Can't Go Home Again" was "a truism, maybe a biblical phrase," but not a weighty novel.

More damning, many think the Thomas Wolfe Memorial honors that other Tom Wolfe—the white-suited journalist and author of books like *Bonfire of the Vanities* and *The Right Stuff.*

Mark Boyd is a creative-writing major in his twenties who likes reading the classics. The son of a friend, he moved to Asheville when he decided to take time off from school and I have known him for years. When I called him a year ago to say I was in town, I asked him to dinner so I could hear his thoughts on Wolfe. "I know that he wrote *The Electric Kool-Aid Acid Test*," he told me on the phone, "but I have never read it." Wrong Wolfe.

One of my current college students told me that when he was in high school, his teacher assigned a Wolfe short story and gave her class a little introduction to its author. "Now my teacher was a good woman, but not the brightest," he said, recalling that her introduction of the writer's life created a composite of the two Wolfes. According to the teacher, "Thomas Wolfe wrote these books of the thirties and also wrote books about drugs and the stock market."

When I share these anecdotes with Chris Morton, Interpretations Manager at the Wolfe Memorial, he laughs so hard, he doubles over at the waist. "Happens all the time," he says, smiling. "Recently, after a forty-five-minute tour of the house, I took the group back out on the porch and asked if anyone had questions. This one lady raises her hand and asked, 'When did he start wearing the white suit?'"

Back when he was alive, when people talked about the greats of the day, the following names were often grouped together: Hemingway, Fitzgerald, Faulkner, and Wolfe.

That suited Thomas Wolfe just fine. He wanted fame. He wanted it so badly he would stay up all night writing and then wander the streets of New York in a daze, proclaiming to passersby, "I wrote ten thousand words today!" Wolfe worked on his first novel, originally titled *O Lost*, for three years. It would become *Look Homeward, Angel*, a story about a boy named Eugene Gant, who grows up in the mountain town of Altamont, North Carolina, a place he mostly hates for its provinciality. He also hates his alcoholic father and his cold, calculating mother, who runs a boarding-house. So he leaves town for college, and then Boston.

Wolfe wrote the book while in the midst of the long-term affair with Aline Bernstein, twenty years his senior, and Jewish (despite Wolfe's being somewhat of an anti-Semite). Wolfe was Bernstein's protégé; she his mother figure. She helped him write, and helped him find a publisher when he completed his 1,113-page, nearly 330,000-word manuscript. Bernstein sent it to Boni & Liveright, the press that at the time published Theodore Dreiser and Dorothy Parker, among others, while Wolfe waited anxiously. The publishers rejected the manuscript for, among other concerns, being, "so long—so terribly long."

Bernstein then sent it to a literary agent, Madeleine Boyd. Boyd spent all night reading the book; at three in the morning, she ran through her apartment screaming, "A genius! I have discovered a genius!"

Despite her regard for his work, Boyd was not fond of her new client.

She told Wolfe he "needed to take a bath" and let him know that she would not sleep with him, though he crowed that all women wanted to. Still, they worked together. Boyd sent *Look Homeward, Angel* to several publishers, who, like Boni & Liveright, rejected it as "fearfully diffuse," "terrible," and of "elephantine length." In 1928, when Boyd "shrewdly maneuvered" Maxwell Perkins into asking for the manuscript, the legendary Scribner's editor was also working with Hemingway and Fitzgerald. Scribner's signed up Wolfe in January of the following year, and Perkins took a very active role in shaping the manuscript.

Perkins suggested that Wolfe alter some of the characters so they didn't so closely resemble the real-life counterparts they were based upon. According to David Herbert Donald's biography, Wolfe told the editor he could not do it: "He had described the people exactly as they were." It was then that Perkins realized Wolfe's book was "often literally autobiographical—that these people in it were his people." He forced Wolfe to change all the real names to fictional ones, for fear of libel suits. Wolfe would often complain about Perkins's intervention, telling Boyd, "Those sons of bitches, they are taking the balls off me!"

When the book came out in October 1929, Scribner's heavily promoted it, even displaying the cover in the window of its Manhattan building. Wolfe loved the attention: "[He] walked back and forth in front of the window so regularly that he drew the attention of the police and came close to being arrested," writes Carol Ingalls Johnston in *Of Time and the Artist: Thomas Wolfe, His Novels, and the Critics*. He checked on bookstores, too, to see if people were buying it.

Wolfe's first reviews came from back home in Asheville. A friend praised the new work in one newspaper, while another paper panned it, stating that most of the characters were real people, portrayed harshly, and that folks in Asheville would be able to identify those whom Wolfe was pillorying: "If there attaches to them any scandal which has enjoyed only a subterranean circulation, it is dragged forth into the light." A third local paper critiqued Wolfe's crudity and titled its review "Former Asheville Writer Turns in Fury upon N.C. and the South."

The controversy, however, made *Look Homeward, Angel* a sensation in Asheville, where it sold well and angered a number of readers. "The boy should be spanked for his impertinence," a bank director said of Wolfe. Even more attacks focused on the book's earthiness, the "bad" language and sexual content. Townspeople began to look differently at Julia Wolfe, who was particularly hurt by her portrayal in the book. However, since the book was so successful, she also took pride in her son, whom she referred to as "the only Asheville author who ever sold one hundred thousand copies." (*Look Homeward, Angel* sold a similar number of copies as its contemporary, *The Sound and the Fury* by William Faulkner, though its sales were far below another publication of the same year: Hemingway's *A Farewell to Arms*.)

Wolfe was upset by the harsh reaction in Asheville. He had hoped to make a name for himself in his town—a goal he accomplished, but it was a name usually reviled. He imagined a future in which: "the same people who now criticized [me] would be building monuments to me, comparing me to O. Henry (hah!), naming their children after me, and nigger children too (hah!), and stuffing me with food, just so they can get a good look at me, and tell of my great contribution to the great literature of the South (hah!)."

In New York, though, Wolfe was a darling of the literati. But fame can pinch back. Wolfe complained to Fitzgerald that he was being made into a cliché—everybody insisted on picturing him:

> as a great "exuberant" six-foot-six clod-hopper straight out of nature who bites off half a plug of apple tobacco, tilts the corn liquor jug and lets half of it gurgle down his throat, wipes off his mouth with the back of one hairy paw, jumps three feet in the air and clacks his heels together four times before he hits the floor again and yells out "Whoopee, boys, I'm a rootin, tootin, shootin son of a gun from Buncombe County—out of my way now, here I come!"—and then wads up three-hundred thousand words or so, hurls it at a blank page, puts covers on it and says, "Here's my book!"

Wolfe was no idiot savant, as is clear to readers of the book, but highly though idiosyncratically educated, having read deeply at home, but also having studied at the University of North Carolina and Harvard.

In Asheville, Wolfe received at least as many negative reviews for *Look Homeward, Angel* as positive ones. Literary scholars seeking to salvage his reputation today argue for classifying *Look Homeward, Angel* as an autobiography. The late essayist and novelist William Styron summed up Wolfe's style this way: "Wolfe, though superbly gifted at imaginative projection, was practically incapable of extended dramatic invention, his creative process being akin to the setting into motion of some marvelous mnemonic tape recorder deep within his cerebrum, from which he unspooled reel after reel of the murmurous, living past."

Chris Morton is not a fan of Wolfe's writing, a fact he's surprisingly up front about. An Asheville native, he read *Look Homeward, Angel*, "out of a sense of obligation," then in college, he enrolled in an American literature course. One of the books on the syllabus was Wolfe's 720-page tome *You Can't Go Home Again*.

"It was huge!" he recalls. "I thought, 'I'm not doing this,' and dropped the course."

Spending the last ten years working at the Thomas Wolfe Memorial has not changed Morton's view of Wolfe: "I don't like much of his work. I have struggled to read his lesser-known novels. He was an undisciplined writer."

Visitation numbers at the Memorial are "unhealthy," Morton tells me. The house was partially burned down a few years ago by an arsonist. The fire destroyed the dining room completely, and damaged 30 percent of the structure in addition to melting or burning up two hundred artifacts. The house closed down for six years, from 1998 to 2004, and it cost $2.4 million to restore it. (The culprit was never found.) The staff kept the visitors' center open during all the years the house was shuttered for renovations; maybe five thousand to six thousand people came each year. When the Old Kentucky Home reopened in 2004 as the Thomas Wolfe Memorial, there was a surge in visits. But, last summer, they only had about nine thousand tourists, roughly a quarter of the people who examined the Memorial before the fire. Morton is working very hard to figure out ways to get more people in, but another question lurks, I suspect, in the back of his head. Maybe the whole thing should be shut down?

Wolfe's obsessive realism makes the Thomas Wolfe House one of the few writers' homes that achieves its aim: The restored boardinghouse provides the autobiographical context for scenes from his fiction.

Thomas Wolfe did not live in this house—if we consider "living in a house" to be an experience of conventional domesticity, meaning parents and children sleeping in their rooms every night. Julia Wolfe bought the boardinghouse in 1906, when she realized her alcoholic husband, William Oliver (W. O.) Wolfe, would no longer be able to support the family. She was a shrewd businesswoman, eager to gain financially. Julia forced her son Thomas—the youngest of her eight children—into the family business, sending him to the railway station in the afternoons to pass out advertising cards for the house. When you take a tour of the house today, you receive a reproduction of these cards. "Block From Square Or Post Office," it reads. "Newly Furnished Throughout. Rates Reasonable. No Sick People." Wolfe and his seven brothers and sisters floated between W.O.'s home, a few blocks away, and the boardinghouse. Wolfe never had his own room; he slept in whichever room had not been let for the night. He hated the boardinghouse, and he disliked his absent, abusive father and his bottom-line-obsessed mother.

The Thomas Wolfe Memorial does not move us to think about the creative spirit so much as it moves us to think about everyday life. Cleave it from its ties to literary celebrity and it becomes replete in and of itself: Come see how, in a certain place in a certain time, some people lived, and some made a living.

And these were not fancy people. The Wolfe home offers a stark contrast to Asheville's primary tourist attraction: the Biltmore Estate, the late nineteenth-century sprawling summer home of the über-rich Vanderbilt family. "This place is not wholly unfamiliar to most visitors; coming here is not like going to the Biltmore," Chris Morton tells me. "How can you relate to the Vanderbilt family? You can relate to the struggles of Eugene Gant. It's a timeless story. It's a story of adolescence that all of us at some point get through."

Morton is jealous but good-naturedly derisive of the Biltmore pitch: "Come See America's Largest Home." "I mean, anyone can say, 'Let's load the kids up and see America's largest house, honey,'" Morton tells me. "They get people there all year long, even for the Festival of Flowers, which takes place at the estate when there really aren't that many flowers in bloom."

Asheville is funky and lovely, if perhaps a bit smug and pleased with itself in that way of small, liberal cities. The enclave formed by the mountains around it only reinforces the charm and provincialism of the place. It's a literate place, too: in this age of blogs, 'zines still proliferate. At Malaprop's, the independent bookstore that serves as a social hub for the city, the coffee shop drinks are named after writers. You can order an Anaïs Nin, an Isabel Allende, or a Gail Godwin. The Walt Whitman is a macadamia nut latte.

Plenty of people buy Wolfe's books, according to the clerk at Malaprop's, especially tourists and "people thinking about moving here." Of course, buying a book and reading it are two different things. A woman I met who moved to Asheville five years ago told me she has started "those damned novels seven, eight times and can never get through them," before proclaiming with exasperation: "All that description. God!"

Today, among critics and academics, it is slightly embarrassing to admit to liking Thomas Wolfe. The conventional thinking is that he has appeal to some adolescent males, but that's it. As Kurt Vonnegut wrote: "I enjoyed *Look Homeward, Angel* when I read it at the age of twenty-two or so. I read the novels in the order they were written, and lost enthusiasm before I reached the end of *You Can't Go Home Again.* I have not dipped into any of the books since, nor have I found myself wishing that Wolfe had lived longer so that I might have more of his work to read. I outgrew him, perhaps."

Alfred Kazin calls Wolfe the "Tarzan of rhetoric," adding that, "[He] pilfered recklessly from the Jacobeans and Sir Thomas Browne, James Joyce and Swinburne, Gilbert Murray and the worst traditions of Southern oratory, was a gluttonous English instructor's accumulation." Robert Penn Warren calls Wolfe "sometimes grand" but "more often tedious and tinged with hysteria."

William Styron finds Wolfe a "bothersome presence." He writes, "[He] refuses to fit gracefully and inevitably into any niche we have reserved on the face of that edifice memorializing Great American Writers." His critical standing, Styron continues, "which has always been shaky, and the grave unevenness of the work itself—torrentially powerful, nervously alive and radiant, at its best; at its worst, sophomoric, hyperinflated and tediously repetitive—have persistently kept Wolfe out of the Valhalla where we have enshrined the leading writers of his generation: Faulkner, Hemingway and Fitzgerald."

Most criticism—whether praising or damning—focuses on Wolfe's ambition to sum up all experience. You can see this on the walls of the Wolfe Memorial's exhibit hall, in glass: quotations from still-famous writers are hung as you enter the exhibit, as if to convince you that this Wolfe was indeed a great American writer: "Wolfe tried to do the greatest of the impossible . . . to reduce all human experience to literature" (Faulkner); "Wolfe was wonderful and unsurpassable" (Hemingway). "A great talent, a very fine delicate spirit." (Hemingway's criticism owes nothing to his "book-jacket-like" praise. It was known that Hemingway also called Wolfe "a one book boy and a glandular giant with the brains and the guts of three mice.") "Who was the greatest writer? Wolfe! Thomas Wolfe. After me, of course" (Kerouac); "*Look Homeward, Angel* was my spawning ground, my birthplace, and my cradle" (Pat Conroy). Conroy goes on: "While reading that fabulous book, I learned that there was a connection between literature and ecstasy. I had been waiting my whole life for Wolfe to present himself to me. My writing career began the instant I finished *Look Homeward, Angel.* Thomas Wolfe taught me that the great books change you immediately and forever."

Morton is good-looking in a southern preppy way. He sports a light blue polo shirt, khakis, and brown-leather loafers. He has clear green eyes and a distinguished widow's peak in his brown hair. He lives with his wife and two small children in Buncombe County. He is calm and smart. He has a remarkable and soothing talent for story-telling. Morton sees no conflict between his view of Wolfe and his job. "There's an assumption that if you work here you're a Wolfe scholar or fan, but that does not apply to me," he says. "The novels are high, lofty, flowery narratives. As a lyricist, his prose is beautiful—it's always easy for me to find a good quote for a Chamber of Commerce newsletter. But Wolfe does not speak to me." What does speak to Morton is public history. His father and grandfather worked for the National Park Service, and his dad took Chris on trips to other parks. "I loved how gifted interpreters—gifted storytellers—could bring a place to life. They could take these stagnant things and, through the senses, make them come to life." His father nurtured his son's ambition by planning vacations to various national parks and historic sites, like Colonial Williamsburg and Gettysburg.

In college, Morton didn't want to teach in a conventional setting, though he did get a teaching certificate, and worked at historic sites in the area. All those experiences make him well-suited to maintaining the relevance of the Thomas Wolfe Memorial. "It is my hope that I can present a story that can engage the visitors, to pull in influences of this little small town and this situation that he grew up in. In so many of these historic sites, you come away with static figures. I want to make them real and very three-dimensional. I want visitors to know that they can relate to what happened in this house."

A Morton-led tour of the Wolfe Memorial conjures two authorial presences—Wolfe's and Morton's. Both know how to set a scene. In Julia's bedroom, Morton showed through words her complicated relationship with W. O., and I imagined, based on their inward looking gazes, that some of my fellow tour-goers were reflecting on their complicated marriages as he spoke. At the end of the tour, Morton led us into the room in which Wolfe wrote "Return," an account of his first trip back to Asheville after the publication of *Look Homeward, Angel*. Morton slowed his delivery and shifted his tone. Gone were the anecdotes about Julia and clever quips about the boarders who stayed in the odd collection of small bedrooms. Morton grew quiet, and sadness deepened his voice. He explained how Wolfe, prodigal son, returned to Asheville and to the house that gave him material and pain. It was 1937, one year before his death. Morton gestured to the copy of "Return" on the desk and had us gather around the small pamphlet. Inside, Wolfe describes what it was like for him to tour his childhood "home" as an adult:

> And all of it is as it has always been: again, again, I turn, and find again the things that I have always known: the cool sweet magic of starred mountain night, the huge attentiveness of dark, the slope, the street, the trees, the living silence of the houses waiting, and the fact that April has come back again. . . . And again, again, in the old house I feel beneath my tread the creak of the old stair, the worn rail, the whitewashed walls, the feel of darkness and the house asleep, and think, "I was a child here; here the stairs, and here was darkness; this was I, and here is Time."

Reading these words in this house and on this tour, it is hard not to be just a bit transported, and to forgive Wolfe his excesses.

Morton's tour is an ephemeral work of art, a narrative that rises and falls as we climb and descend the old stairs. But not enough people show up to take it. "Maybe it is Wolfe's diminished stature," Morton speculates about the lack of interest. "There's nothing to motivate the average museum-goer to come here." Last summer, to help determine how to attract more people, the staff asked visitors to complete a survey about their reasons for stopping by.

Wolfe could have become a cult favorite like William S. Burroughs or Charles Bukowski, other alienated writers loved by male adolescents. Asheville could be like Lawrence, Kansas, is to followers of Burroughs, a mecca for Wolfeans. With its drop-out charm and teeming, underemployed twenty-somethings, the town is well-positioned for stoner pilgrimages to Wolfe's house. But those fanatics who exist tend to be older, like the members of the Thomas Wolfe Society, a group of admirers that publish the *Thomas Wolfe Review,* and are responsible for about 80 percent of the scholarship on the widely forgotten author.

Wolfe followers do show up at the Memorial. Morton calls them "Gushers." These idolizers—men, usually—consider him the greatest American writer, ever. Gushers love what many hate about Wolfe's prose: its intense, rambling mysticism. And, yes, Wolfe tries to trap the whole of experiences in his sentences. Here is the second line from *Look Homeward, Angel:* "Each of us is all the sums he has not counted: subtract us into nakedness and night again, and you shall see begin in Crete four thousand years ago the love that ended yesterday in Texas." Morton says that Gushers occasionally come from the literary crowd, but the author also tends to attract misfits: "Wolfe seems to be appealing to the class of folks who don't fit in, who feel alienated from their families, communities."

The Gushers seek out Morton and the staff of the Memorial for their expertise on Wolfe. One in particular, a German man, e-mailed Morton in a seemingly desperate attempt to track down recommendations for a biography on Wolfe, after his local booksellers proved unhelpful. "Our conversation ultimately turned to the fact of Wolfe's diminished stature," Morton recalls. "And, of course, my German friend simply could not believe that this would be the case in the U.S. To me, in the tone of his e-mails, I heard a man who, having heard 'a voice in the chaos of the man swarm,' as Wolfe called it, had lost it and was desperately and frantically seeking someone who could help him find it once again."

While I was sitting in Malaprop's at my laptop, the man sitting next to me and I get to talking, and he turned out to the purest example of a Gusher: one who credits Thomas Wolfe with changing his life.

Tom Mahon is a businessman from Saratoga Springs, in Upstate New York. He's a noticeable guy, the kind who looks vaguely famous. He's lean, with a lined face, a head of white hair and blue eyes so intense you can't look into them. He's traveling through Asheville, he says, on a long trip without an itinerary. At its end, he will relocate to New York City to try to make living as an actor.

At this particular moment, however, Mahon is my literary guide, explaining to me Wolfe's genius, and his own devotion to the writer. "He was excessive, that's one of the grandest things about him. Wolfe records things the way Hemingway never did. I love his 'bombosity,' his voluptuousness. He's embedded in a culture, embedded in people. He had the tempo of the blood. There's something Wolfean about him."

We talk for two hours. Or, rather, he talks, narrating in precise language—combined with asides—Wolfe's place within twentieth-century literature and the story of his own life. I listen, transfixed.

"He writes about the wonder of being alive, people to love, people to hate, all these things. He was much more interested in Hugo, Goethe, and that whole sweep. Wolfe took the whole, that Whitman maxim, you know, just go along, first thing to do is to get it down and then go through it all. Wolfe had an intangible no other writer had. Fitzgerald didn't have it. Hemingway didn't have it."

Mahon discovered Wolfe in college. Mahon had been reading Dylan Thomas, and he got a copy of his poems and he couldn't believe, as Thomas says, "the goings on on paper." After Thomas, Mahon read Wolfe and felt the same. "I was like, 'What the heck?' And the way he was using language was to me fascinating."

"It's a misnomer to call it falling in love. It's more like a rising in love. The more I read, the more I saw how daring you could be in language. I couldn't believe how great it was."

Mahon left college for Vietnam. He took *Look Homeward, Angel* with him, reading it late into the night, then getting up at four A.M. to keep reading. He read passages to the soldiers in his company, but none of his Army buddies were interested.

I ask Mahon if he's gone to the old boardinghouse. No, he says. I ask him if he would, and let me know what he thinks. Six months later, I get an e-mail: "I didn't get to the house, but no regrets," he writes. "I had an up-and-down excursion in Asheville. So did Wolfe. I imagined he was looking down and feeling he'd accomplished something after all, and probably laughed when I did, and caught his breath when I did, and his eyes moistened when mine did."

Chris Morton tells me that he'd hoped traffic through the Thomas Wolfe Memorial would pick up in 2000, the centennial of the author's birth: A stamp was issued by the post office. The original manuscript of *Look Homeward, Angel* was published, and some biographies came out, too. None brought a Wolfe resurgence. Then Wolfe was left off the Modern Library's 100 Best Novels list. "They said that they might put it back in," says Morton, "but that's even more insulting. It's like, 'Oops, we forgot about him.'"

With no bump from the centennial, Morton hopes that by reinterpreting the site, he can draw more of a crowd. For one, he'd like to eliminate "the shrine aspect"—which might make the house more accessible to people other than the Gushers—adding that he wants to change the name from the Thomas Wolfe Memorial to something less monumental. "Maybe we limit ourselves because we don't offer choices to visitors," Morton says, musing out loud. "I mean, do people really want to spend two hours of their day vacationing in Asheville at the house of a writer they've never read?"

Morton also thinks that placing the house in the context of early twentieth-century Asheville would make it more appealing to visitors, though he acknowledges that Wolfe's story cannot be abandoned: "There are more stories here that need to be fleshed out, such as the rise to prominence of Asheville," he says. "The boardinghouses that are all gone. We think of them as flophouses, but boardinghouses were the forerunners of the bed-and-breakfast. They were typically run by women. This was a very typical, mainstream, ordinary family. It had in its midst a genius. Visitors find that story interesting."

Maybe the problem is not that people do not come to the Thomas Wolfe Memorial, but that the Memorial was created in the first place. The boardinghouse was sold after Wolfe's mother died in 1945, only a few years after his own death, when his reputation was at its height. Since 1949, the house has been kept as a memorial. Perhaps we got ahead of ourselves in the literary-canon game. God did not hand down a list of literary masterpieces on a stone tablet, after all. The canon of American literature is man-made and mutable. What we consider "classic" differs from generation to generation as critical tastes and readerships evolve. In his book on canon formation, the literary scholar Henry Louis Gates satirized the misconception that classics are picked by a "man up there" doing the dirty work of picking and choosing the greats: "There's no immortality in this business. You want twenty years, even forty, we can arrange it. Beyond that, we'll have to renegotiate terms at the end of the period. Sooner or later there's going to be a, whaddaya call it, reassessment. We send a guy down, he does an appraisal, figures the reputation's not really earned, and bingo, you're out. Maybe you'll get a callback in fifty years or so. Maybe not."

Maybe Wolfe will never get a callback. Maybe Max Perkins made a literary star by pushing hard and got people to chalk him up, wrongly, on the side of the greats. And since it is onerously difficult and expensive to dismantle a historic state house, maybe Chris Morton is doomed to endlessly trying to figure out how to get people to visit the historic state park.

"Some think the house should be a marketing outlet—that it is up to us to promote Wolfe as a great American author, to get his reputation back up again, if he and the museum are going to survive," says Morton. "I don't see it that way: My responsibility is to interpret his life and writing and give people an understanding of the influences on his life. I don't need to be his advocate and promoter. Wolfe's writing needs to stand or fall on its own."

Whether he likes it or not, Morton has become a latter-day Max Perkins. He is trying to create an accessible narrative out of Wolfe's life and writing, to prune and rearrange the house he curates, and to provide the representative examples of Wolfe's prose on the tours. He's doing for Wolfe what Wolfe couldn't do himself, perhaps because he was, as Mahon put it, so "Wolfean."

Wandering around the house with Morton, listening to him shape history, I imagine the great tours he could be giving at Colonial Williamsburg.

Wolf House

Chapter 7

Best-Laid Plans at Jack London State Historic Park

> Your small house, too, in ruin!
> Its feeble walls the winds are scattering!
> And nothing now, to build a new one,
> Of coarse grass green!
> —Robert Burns, "To a Mouse"

THAT READING IS A FORM of escape is a truism. We escape, retreat, surrender into books. They offer us a home away from home (especially when home is unwanted); they grant us immersion. The Oxford Dictionary defines this absorption through the act of reading: "*she was totally absorbed in her book.* ENGROSS IN, captivate by, occupy with, preoccupy with, engage in, rivet by, grip by, hold by, interest in, immerse in, involve in, enthrall by, spellbound by, fascinate by/with."

Writing is a form of escape, too. The quest for absorption is also what moves many to write. In his essay "Why Write?" Alan Shapiro describes the pleasure that writing provides as "perfectly useless concentration." We write, Shapiro tells us, "for the total immersion of the experience, the narrowing and intensification of focus to the right here, right now, the deep joy of bringing the entire soul to bear upon a single act of concentration." Saul Bellow says something similar: "I think that art has something to do with an arrest of attention in the midst of distraction."

In fact, when we write, we are not even ourselves: "It is self-forgetful even if you are writing about the self, because you yourself have disappeared into the pleasure of making: your identity—the incessant, transient, noisy New York Stock Exchange of desires and commitments, ambitions, hopes, hates, appetites, and interests—has been obliterated by the rapture of complete attentiveness. In that extended moment, opposites cohere: the mind feels and the heart thinks, and receptivity's a form of fierce activity. Quotidian distinctions between mind and body, self and other, space and time, dissolve."

In other words, writing provides the same pleasure of forgetfulness one experiences one-third of the way through a great novel.

A visit to a writer's house can be a way to get out of yourself, too. But the action that leads a house to be preserved—the production of words by the writer who lived there—is an act of absorption itself—an escape from, say, household worries. This paradox—by escaping the mundane somebody did something so profound that the mundane is what we now revere—is central to my skepticism about writers' houses.

At the same time, a trip to a writer's house—and the act of writing—can be as much an act of narcissism as it is an escape from self. How might I become like this great writer? Can I pick up any hints? Does my house look as good as this one? And of course, the one that lurks behind all other questions—maybe even my own interest in these houses—what will happen to me after I am gone? For what will I be remembered? Who will do the remembering? Will anyone want to preserve *my* house?

Similarly, the theory of writing as euphoria—a selfless ecstasy—only gets at part of why writers write. Another part is seemingly opposite and embarrassingly crass: a desire for immortality. As a writer myself, I must admit to being somewhat confused by dancers and stage actors and chefs. All that work, I think, all that practice and preparation and effort, for what? An ephemeral product, an hour or two on stage, a meal to be eaten? How does one put so much into something that will only dissipate and dissolve into the slipstream of unreliable memory? Writers choose words as their métier partially out of a desire for the solid permanence that publication, reading, and rereading provide.

A hope for immortality is at stake when we lose ourselves in art. But tragically we are unable to arrest the future, to ensure permanence. Whitman could not control the posthumous objects he hoped would preserve his legacy—the tombstone with the wrong date, the brain that splattered on the floor. "The thought of death" was not "merged in the thought of materials" quite as he wanted them to. Nor were they for Hemingway or Wolfe, who also tried but failed to have us heed their directions.

Writers—devoted to a craft based in absorption—also have a strong link to depression. It may be that depression, a state of constant distraction, is a precondition for the "arrest of attention" that absorption, and art, provide. I have visited many authors' museums that housed intense sadness. Sometimes writers' houses offer us a space to contemplate an author's attempt to secure his own immortality, the ego driving, the future vainly predicted. No house better exemplifies this too human vanity than Jack London State Historic Park in California.

Jack London was a restless, depressive self-made man, and he devoted most of his final years to building a ranch. In 1913, he wrote to a friend about his place in Sonoma Valley, California: "Come to see what I am trying to do with the soil, and with hogs, and with beef-cattle, and dairy-cows, and draft-horses." Who knew? Jack London, the macho, womanizing, alcoholic, adventure-traveler public celebrity spent the last years of his short life building a humane "Pig Palace" for his livestock and pouring manure down a slope so as to avoid using chemicals. London was best known then, as he is now, as a writer. But he was obsessed by the question of his legacy and his posthumous future. He wanted to be known after his death, and he did not want to be known for his writing. He wanted it to be for his ranch and to improve the soil on the land. He pioneered what we would call today sustainable agriculture on his Beauty Ranch, a 1,400-acre farm in Glen Ellen, California.

Today, the ranch, which comprises the Jack London State Historic Park, wreaks havoc with stereotypes. By the time he settled at Glen Ellen in 1905, London was sick of writing, tired of the demands that editors made of him to churn out the types of adventure stories that made him famous. But writing was his meal ticket and the only means he had to earn money for his ranch. So he pushed himself to write a thousand words a day, every day, to raise money for soil and stone. "Do you realize that I devote two hours a day to writing and ten to farming?" he wrote in his journal. "My work on this land, and my message to America, go hand in hand."

He started small, buying 130 acres of land for $7,000. "I believe the soil is our one indestructible asset," London said of his decision to buy the land. "They are 130 acres of the most beautiful, primitive land to be found in California. There are great redwoods on it, some of them thousands of years old—in fact, the redwoods are as fine and magnificent as any to be found anywhere outside the tourist groves."

He built a barn, and bought horses, a cow, a plow, chickens, a buggy, and other farming livestock and equipment. London also kept cranking out prose—sloppy stories that do not hold up to his earlier masterpieces, such as *The Call of the Wild*, which had made him an instant literary celebrity.

When he cleared forty acres and tried to raise hay, he discovered the land had been stripped by generations of "old-fashioned methods of taking everything off and putting nothing back." Jack wanted to succeed where the previous ranchers had failed. He saw his work as part and parcel of his socialist politics: "In the solution of the great economic problems of the present age, I see a return to the soil. I go into farming because my philosophy and research have taught me to recognize the fact that a return to the soil is the basis of economics."

In his obsessive, restless style—this is, after all, the man who, when deciding he wanted to spend time on a boat, taught himself sailing and navigation and crossed the Pacific in the *Snark*—London, who had never worked the land before, taught himself everything he could about farming, reading agricultural manuals and scientific tomes. "I adopted the policy of taking nothing off the ranch," he said.

He also used techniques he had seen in Korea as a war correspondent: terracing, rotating crops, and using natural fertilizer, "so that instead of one-tenth of one meager crop a year you can grow three rich crops a year." He built the first concrete block silo in California and filled it with silage from his and neighboring ranches. He hired Italian stonemasons to build a barn for his horses, and a manure pit to develop fertilizer.

In 1915, he built the "Pig Palace," a round structure that had feed in the middle and stalls all around. Each sow and her piglets would have their own "apartment" with a sun porch in front, which served as their dining room, and an outside run in back. One man could care for over two hundred hogs, and the opening of one valve filled all the troughs. At first, the nearby ranchers laughed, but the design later earned awards and nationwide attention. Today, many of London's techniques have become standard operating procedure among ranchers.

By his death in 1916, due to either suicide or the side effects of alcoholism (no one is sure), the ranch was one of the largest in Northern California. But, perhaps because he was so ahead of his time—or because he was a distracted, drunk rancher who was often off on sailing adventures and thus neglecting the constant needs of his land—the ranch was an economic failure.

After his death his wife Charmian wrote a plea to posterity, asking his fans to remember "Beauty Ranch" or, as Jack once called it, "The Ranch of Good Intentions." "Have any of you thought what is to become of the great thing he has started up here . . . I am begging you now, with all my heart, not to forget that he laid his hand upon the hills of California." But we have.

In *Virginia Woolf's Nose: Essays on Biography*, Hermione Lee uses the term absorption to get at the allure of biography:

> What makes biography so endlessly absorbing is that through all the documents and letters and witnesses, the conflicting opinions and partial memories and fictionalized versions, we keep catching sight of a real body . . . a physical life: the young Dickens coming quickly into a room, sprightly, long-haired, bright-eyed, dandyish, in a crimson velvet waistcoat or tartan trousers; the sound of Coleridge's voice as he talked magically on and on; Rimbaud, dust-covered and scrawny and dressed in baggy grey khaki trousers, leading a caravan of camels across the desert sands of Abyssinia; Joyce with a black felt hat, thick glasses and a cigar, sitting in Sylvia Beach's bookshop in Paris; Edith Wharton and Henry James, veiled and hatted, tucked up comfortably in the back of the Packard behind the chauffeur, exchanging impressions as they zoom along the empty French roads.

All these are romanticized images, of course. But then death is as much to blame as book-writers for sepia-toning our memories. As Henry James said, death "smoothes the folds" of the beloved: "The figure retained by the memory is compressed and intensified; accidents have dropped away from it and shades have ceased to count; it stands, sharply, for a few estimated and cherished things, rather than nebulously, for a swarm of possibilities."

Writers' houses traffic in those "few and estimated" things. Some are iconic objects, like Balzac's coffeepot in his Paris house. But sometimes the things a writer's house proffers fail to align with our romantic images of the author. At Emily Dickinson's house, the bedside chamber pot smashes many a hoped-for reverie.

London tried too hard to have writing be the distraction, the ranch his absorbing escape and his grab at permanence. He wanted to be remembered for his farming. But it is his books, still crisply in print, and his life, the subject of endless biographies, that we remember. Meanwhile the silo decays.

When I flew to Oakland to visit London's house, I was depressed. My life had taken a sudden, unexpected direction when my husband walked out on me. I was in the midst of an unimagined divorce and faced a future as a single mother. I had no focus, no capacity to become absorbed, no resource with which to forget myself. Except for the garden.

My big old farmhouse in rural Ohio came with 2.6 acres of land, and I found incredible relief and succor in wandering about the fields tinkering with the overly ambitious gardens I had created. I took to the garden the way women before me took cures. I threw seeds on top of the dirt field I created when I replaced the septic tank and started a "wildflower meadow." As many weeds as cornflowers grew, and they were strong, thigh-high, deeply rooted creatures. There was nothing more satisfying than grabbing them low to avoid their prickers, and then pulling them up, hearing those roots break, and flinging the newly dead plant over into the next field. Sometimes I moved big sandstone rocks from one place to another to edge a bed or create a small bench. These blocks were too big for one person to lift alone, but I did so anyway, heedless. I usually ended up dropping them into some inappropriate spot, and then would stand there and look at how wrongly I had placed them, light a cigarette, and then go off to divide some perennials in another bed. I could change my mind as many times as I wanted to—and in that time, I was always changing my mind, stopping mid-bed and wandering off to do something else, because my mind would not stop. There was no end to the options in my garden, and I was alone out there in the field. No one but me cared, and anyway, the plants would keep growing whether I was fastidious or willy-nilly. I was small in the face of my garden, and that was a solace.

Writing and reading, of course, were lost to me, strangers from another life. The morning newspaper required more focus than I could muster in those days. When I flew to Oakland to visit Jack London's house in Glen Ellen, California, I left all my books, biographies, notes, and novels in my suitcase in the overhead compartment. I hoped that the trip would at least be an escape from my inability to escape, from my restless mind.

Beauty Ranch was only one of London's attempts to secure how he would be remembered. There is another one, a house, and like the ranch on which it sits, it also failed to make him his name.

There are actually three houses on the Beauty Ranch property, including the House of Happy Walls, where London lived with his wife and which is now a visitor's center with many displays. There is also a cottage being restored to its appearance during the time the Londons lived there. I spent a long time at both these houses and was captivated by the diorama-type displays of London's typewriter, the letters from the Soviet Union praising London, and the newly restored, but still empty, cottage that the State of California was working to complete. Still, my mind kept leaving the place I was in, drifting off to my son, far away in Ohio, worrying about how difficult it would be to stay up until dark in this Pacific Standard Time town so that I might be able to wish him a good night.

I decided to join a group tour that would take me through the fields to see Beauty Ranch and the third house on the property, Wolf House. Wolf House is not a house but a ruin, a bunch of old stones scattered in the fields at the end of a dirt path framed by redwoods. "My house will be standing, act of God permitting, for a thousand years," London said of this dream house. But the act of God happened brutally fast. The house burned down the day Jack was to move in.

London had hired famed San Francisco architect Albert Farr to build Wolf House in 1911. In another ahead-of-his-time act of sustainability, London used only local materials. He felled redwood trees and then left them in the woods to season. The builders mined volcanic rocks and gathered locally quarried stone. They chose the local materials, in part, to withstand fire damage. "Everyone agreed that rock and concrete, massive beams and redwood logs with the bark on, were practically fireproof unless ignited in a dozen places, owing to the quadrangular construction and cement partitions," London explained. To protect it from an earthquake, the building was put on floating concrete slabs, which were large enough to reinforce a forty-story building.

It was an extravaganza of design and space, as well. The house was four stories tall and had a Spanish tiled roof, a redwood entrance, pergolas, and many porches. All the rafters were left rough-hewn. There was a courtyard with a reflecting pool stocked with local fish. The dining area could accommodate fifty guests, and there was a men-only gaming room. London's study was located in an isolated tower high above the roof. The house had all the then-modern conveniences: hot water, laundry, heating, electric lighting, vacuum and refrigerating plants, a milk room, storeroom, root cellar, and wine cellar.

Carefully designed to avert natural disasters and last a thousand years, it lasted two days. On August 22, 1913, it was engulfed in flames. Speculation raged about whether the blaze was intentional, but proof came more than eighty years later, when, in 1995, a forensic team concluded that oil-soaked rags had spontaneously combusted. Sure it could withstand earthquakes and had stones that could not incinerate, but you never expect a workman to leave a flammable rag behind when he goes home for the day. "It isn't the money loss," London said about the fire. "The main hurt comes form the wanton despoiling of so much beauty."

Some of London's fellow-travelers found the fire karmic—a warning to him for spending so much money on his own castle and not enough on the cash-strapped Socialist Party. London retorted that he built the house with money he had earned only through his labor—the sweat equity of all those mornings writing, a thousand words, no matter what, no matter how good.

The moment our tour group sighted the rocks, we all became quiet and still. Even, thank God, my mind. Wolf House is now nothing more than piles of boulders alone in a field. It is anachronistic, a stone ruin in California. "It looks like something out of *Jane Eyre*," said one visitor who toured the ruins with me. "It looks like something from Europe," said another.

It is sublime in the Burkean sense. In its presence, we all felt both gratifyingly small and distressingly mortal. There you have—jagged and rough and in front of your eyes, yet still somehow sepia-toned and out of time—an ancient relic from the twentieth century. It is what we are looking for when we try to remember, when we try to do justice to the past. But this "ruin" is also alive. The stones that lie at the end of the redwood footpath foster nature, forming ballast for groundcovers and a hideout for rattlesnakes, which our tour guide warned us to be wary of.

Because it cannot be preserved, or restored, or re-created, Wolf House has an authenticity that allows us a glimpse of the visceral, haunting presence that we seem to desire from our writers' houses. Some of us, no doubt, were thinking about our own future death; some reflected on best laid plans. I was triply humbled by London's audacity, by the fire, and, narcissistically, by my own vain attempts to control the future.

All that longing, all that work and then—poof! A fire destroys a man's naked grab at immortality a few scant hours after its completion. That is the stuff of literature. That is the folly of foresight—or the suspension of disbelief that is, say, a wedding vow.

Better to trust the immaterial, that which provides the evidence of things unseen, as the New Testament defines faith, than build houses to our future dead selves. The lyricism of *Leaves of Grass*, the intensity of *The Sun Also Rises*, the heartbreak of *Little Women* remain intact. Our material, our things—gravestones, walls, historically reconstructed objects, even our brains—elude.

The tour was over. After our epiphanies at Wolf House, the three high school friends meeting for a reunion in wine country, the couple from San Francisco on a day trip, and me—alone—walked back through the redwoods to the parking lot. I went to a bar, drank too much locally grown wine, and then went back to my room at the Hilton, where I promptly and thankfully lost consciousness.

Paul Laurence Dunbar House

Chapter 8

The Compensation of Paul Laurence Dunbar

> We need not fear excessive influence. A more generous
> trust is permitted. Serve the great.
> —Ralph Waldo Emerson, "Representative Men"

FOR YEARS, I DROVE AROUND the back roads and small towns of Lorain
County, Ohio, near where I live, looking for old books. There are dozens
of small antique stores. Most of the items for sale are modest by antiquing
standards—a couch for $100; books and lithographs for $30. One or two
shelves of books are usually tucked away in the back. I made some great

finds on these runs—a copy of *Grapes of Wrath* signed by John Steinbeck, a rare first edition of Nathanael West's *A Cool Million*. I bought first editions of George Washington Cable, Albion Tourgee, and Rebecca Harding Davis, writers whose reputations are on the bottom of what I hope to be a "W" curve. The thrill of bringing my nonpecuniary educational background to bear to find something of financial value kept me slightly obsessed.

Once I had them at home I was not sure what I was to do with my purchases, though. Would I fashion myself into a noble book collector adding to literary heritage by preserving these volumes, or would I sell them on eBay, and become a literary entrepreneur? I did a bit of both, and discovered that old books by lesser-known American authors were not the most liquid assets (I unloaded that West first edition for far less than I thought it was worth; the Steinbeck went for more, and no one buys Harding Davis these days, apparently).

I have since stopped browsing dusty shelves in small town antique stores, though I still keep a shelf of books from my forays. My favorite book is a copy of Paul Laurence Dunbar's novel *The Uncalled*. I found the small, dull beige hardback in the corner of a flea market cum antique store, sitting on a low, forgotten shelf. When I opened up the book to look at the price— $35, first edition, written in neat, penciled cursive—I found dozens of clippings pasted inside.

On the inside of the front cover was a bookplate, "Private Library of R. R. Gilbert" with a saying: "Books Are Silent Friends. Use Them Carefully." Then, pasted all over it, were yellowed newspaper clippings. One was from the "Colored" section of the Obituaries. The headline read: "Poet Has Gone To His Lost Home: Paul Lawrence [*sic*] Dunbar, Leading Writer of His Race, Succumbed to Consumption at His Dayton Home, Yesterday." The story gave a thumbnail life of "the poet of the negro race." Another clipping stated that "Paul Lawrence [*sic*] Dunbar may be called the Negro trailblazer of Ohio," and yet another was a response to a reader request to: "Please tell me something about the life of Paul Laurence Dunbar, the Negro Poet." Facing the title page was pasted a clipping featuring a picture of Dunbar's mother, who is sitting in a heavy wooden chair with large armrests. She is wearing a black coat, a hat, and gloves, and is holding a cane. The story below her reads: "Mrs. Matilda Dunbar. Born in slavery, an 86-year-old Dayton mother is now living in the reflected honor an appreciate world is paying to the memory of her son, the late Paul Laurence

Dunbar, Negro poet. In a library lined with her son's books, Mrs. Dunbar often receives his admirers. Each June 27, Dunbar's birthday, his mother holds open house for friends who hear readings from his poetry. The poet, who died at 33, would have been 60 this year, had he lived." The title: "Basks in Dead Poet-Son's Fame."

The purple velvet ribbon used as a bookmark indicated, to me, that R.R. was likely a woman. And so I imagined her—a Daytonian and African American, I inferred—getting her scissors out after reading the newspaper and carefully cutting out Dunbar clippings, before grabbing her copy of *The Uncalled* and pasting them lovingly inside.

This discovery sent me into a series of physical reactions, textbook examples of what we call emotion: adrenaline, heart rate increase, and misty eyes. But here is what floored me even more: there is a twenty-seven-year gap between the earliest and most recent clippings. That means that, over the course of twenty-seven years, R.R. took out her scissors, found her glue, and got out her copy of the novel with earnest devotion. There is so much history and love in this book that I wish I did not possess it. Should it not be someplace else where its story could be told? Where R. R. Gilbert's own story could be shared to help us understand why she documented the posthumous legacy of Dunbar in that book for almost three decades? And it nagged at me, how this book ended up on the bottom shelf of an antique store amidst a few dozen children's books from the 1940s, in LaGrange, Ohio, hundreds of miles north of Dayton.

It is obvious that R.R. loved Dunbar, and Dayton, something fierce. When I finally drove the four hours south from my home to Dayton in order to visit the Paul Laurence Dunbar House, I went with the feeling that I owed it to R.R. to go with the same reverence I found manifest between the pages of our copy of *The Uncalled*.

The Paul Laurence Dunbar House, run by the Ohio Historical Society, was the first state memorial dedicated to an African American. That means that the first time Ohio decided to honor an African American, it did so by creating a writer's house. The home was dedicated in 1936, thirty years after Dunbar's death.

Dunbar's reputation was at its height right before he died. He was dubbed the Negro Poet Laureate of the United States, famous for his dialect poems like "Negro Love Song." He gained much renown, taking part in

William McKinley's inauguration, working for Frederick Douglass and befriending Booker T. Washington and W. E. B. Du Bois.

His reputation, however, took a dive around the time of the Harlem Renaissance. His dialect poems, seen as path-breaking earlier in the century, were lambasted as Uncle Tom-ish. In Cleveland, just a few hours away from Dunbar's hometown and where I live, many have not heard of him. He is perhaps best known today as the originator of the line "I know why the caged bird sings," which Maya Angelou borrowed from his poem "Sympathy" for the title of her autobiography. However, few are aware of the reference, thinking Angelou penned it herself.

The years since Dunbar's death have not been kind to Dayton, either. In 1906, Dayton was "like Vienna," as LaVerne Sci, site manager of the Paul Laurence Dunbar State Memorial, puts it. It was the patent capital of the country, a town on the make. Orville and Wilbur Wright were there, and helped draw other inventors to the area. It was a precursor to the Silicon Valleys of the world, acting as an important site for the groundbreaking endeavors of scientists and engineers, particularly those involved with the Manhattan Project.

Today, Dayton is a struggling rust belt town searching for a new motto to replace "patent capital." Its population has been declining since the 1970s. The city remains largely segregated. The per capita income is about $15,000 a year, and about 23 percent of the population has an income below the poverty level. And rather than spawn innovation, it's more focused on preserving its past. In 2003, the National Park Service renovated the Dayton Aviation Heritage Trail, which commemorates Dunbar, as well as Wilbur and Orville Wright. (Dunbar went to high school with the Wrights, and they were friends.) The Wright Cycle Company building and print shop have been restored along with the Wright Brothers Aviation Center. But despite what I am sure are high hopes, scads of committee meanings, and the best intentions of civic leaders, Wright-Dunbar tourism does not seem to be altering the fate of this dying city.

I arrived in Dayton on an early October day already suffering from the kind of inhospitable, gray fifty-degree weather that makes Daytonians dream of Daytona Beach. I was staying in one of the city's few hotels, the Crowne Plaza, right downtown. I needed directions from there to the Dunbar house, so I asked the concierge. "The what house?" he said, looking surprised.

"The Paul Laurence Dunbar House," I answered. "He was a poet who lived here."

Still clueless, the concierge took out his map. I showed him the neighborhood where the house was located. He called over Bill, the shuttle driver, to consult.

It was only ten on a Sunday morning, and the house didn't open until noon. So I asked Bill, who had never been to the Dunbar House, to drive me by it, so that I knew where it was, and then to drop me off at the open Wright-Dunbar Aviation Center. "I'm not sure you want to walk from *here* to *there*," he said as we pulled up to the house.

By "here," he meant the ghetto. And by "there," Bill was referring to the street just three blocks away, on which the Aviation Center sits, and which had been dandied up to look all old-timey and quaint for the tourists. Just as he said this, we watched three black kids, maybe ten years old, run around the corner, laughing and playing. I told him I'd be fine.

Dunbar chose this neighborhood when he moved back to his hometown in 1904. He was thirty-one and about to die. He wanted to live out his last days in Dayton, and to ensure the well-being of his mother, who would outlive him for thirty years. At that time, Miami Valley, Dayton's first suburb, was new, up and coming, and full of promise. Today, the neighborhood is neither this nor that: boarded-up houses sit next to nicely preserved ones with mums sprinkled around their foundations. The only open businesses, when I was there at least, were a pawnshop and a Subway restaurant. And the crisp blue banner announcing the "Wright-Dunbar Historic Business District" made me melancholy. I have seen so many of these banners in Cleveland, where I currently live, and in Philadelphia, where I used to live. I know all too well that happy, bright banners like that are heralds of desperation. They announce what I suspect will be yet another failed urban renewal project.

Still, the Aviation Center does a wonderful job chronicling Dayton's history, as well as the story of the Wright Brothers and Dunbar's poetry. Unfortunately, few come to take in its completeness. The gift shop carries some Dunbar titles, but not many, because, according to the Park Ranger, the publisher's minimum order quantity is more copies than they can sell.

Dunbar is more obscure now than when he was alive, and Dayton has shrunk in size and reputation. A double whammy. When I visit the lesser-known houses of lesser-known authors—where there is no majestic beauty to distract you while you contemplate ruins, as in Glen Ellen, or great restaurant to check out after your tour, as in Asheville—I feel a compensatory responsibility to call attention to the house, to take some action, to redress the neglect.

At these houses my faith is restored. There is purpose here precisely because they honor the overlooked. And that they do so within a house becomes somehow suitable and honest, because houses are not, by definition, monuments. They are small, private places fit for someone whose reputation is diminishing and becoming ever more private. They are, in many ways, the institutional equivalents of R.R. Gilbert's copy of *The Uncalled*. Precious yet forgotten: attention should be paid.

Unfortunately, there are few houses in honor of historically underrepresented writers, because they have been, well, historically underrepresented, and thus their houses historically underpreserved.

"Don't ever think that rap is something new. Dunbar put rhythm in words long ago," LaVerne Sci says. Sci, the site manager of the Paul Laurence Dunbar State Memorial, is finishing a mesmerizing thirty-minute introduction to the life and works of Dunbar. I'm sitting in the auditorium of the visitors' center with seven others who have come for the Sunday afternoon tour. Sci knows how to enthrall the audience. She performs. This is no dry recounting of birthdates and names. It's a one-woman show. Sometimes her eyes shut as she tries to remember what to say next, but her monologue isn't canned. She impersonates slave masters, parodies Dunbar's critics, and compares Reconstruction-era African American families to New Orleanians displaced by Katrina (it was only a month after the hurricane hit when I visited).

Before she begins the tour of the house, she finishes her performance with one last anecdote: "Dunbar went to this restaurant to get a job and when he walked in the door he notices the waiters," she starts. "They were all black. And as they were serving the tables, they were talking over their shoulders to each other about their romantic exploits. He notices the waiters would come from the kitchen through the swinging doors carrying their hot dishes and the hot coffee. They'd push that door open and they'd say 'Jump back, Honey! Jump back!'"

Sci then readies us for a bit of call and response. "So we're going to do his 'Negro Love Song,'" she warns us. "Every time I do like this" (she throws her hands toward the audience), "I want you to say, 'Jump Back, Honey.' Let's practice."

Sci throws her hands toward us.

Jump Back Honey, we mumble rather pathetically.

"Oh, no. This is the Dunbar house. Oh no. With enthusiasm."

Jump Back Honey, we try with a bit more life.

"Still not enthusiastic enough. Now let's say it like we mean it. This is the Dunbar house," she shouts. "Ready, and go!"

Then, she leads us in the chant. "Seen my lady home las' night," she sings, before giving us our cue.

Jump back, honey, jump back, we shout.

"Hel' huh han' and sque'z it tight."

Jump back honey, jump back

"Hyead huh sigh a little sigh,

Seen a light gleam f'om huh eye,

An' a smile go flittin' by"

Jump back, honey, jump back.

"Isn't that cute? And that is so Dunbar." Sci smiles, and ushers us into the house.

Paul is not the protagonist of the Paul Laurence Dunbar House. Matilda, or "Mother Dunbar," as Sci refers to her, takes that crown. She is singularly responsible for the house's existence, Sci says. Matilda made Paul into a writer, and then made sure he was memorialized. Sci is simply carrying on Matilda's legacy, our guide asserts.

Born a slave, Matilda had two children by her master in Shelbyville, Kentucky. After the war, she moved to Dayton to live with her mother. In Dayton, she took on work as a washerwoman. In 1871, she met Joshua Dunbar, who had been enslaved as a plasterer on another Kentucky plantation. His master hired him out, and Joshua squirreled enough money away to buy himself a can of cayenne pepper. He used this pepper to throw the dogs off his tracks when he escaped on the Underground Railroad.

Joshua made it to Canada. He taught himself to read while he was still a slave, and once in Canada he read newspapers, through which he learned about the Civil War. In 1863, at age forty, he joined the 55th Regiment of the Massachusetts Volunteer Infantry. He was medically discharged, but then reenlisted as a cavalryman in 1865. He was medically discharged again, this time at the rank of sergeant, before he moved to Dayton.

Joshua and Matilda's marriage was acrimonious, perhaps due to financial and emotional struggles. In Reconstruction-era Dayton, Joshua couldn't find work. Their second child, Elizabeth, died when she was two years old. The couple fought frequently, and Joshua may have been physically abusive. They divorced in 1876.

Paul was a precocious child. His parents anticipated greatness from him from the day he was born. They taught him with both book learning—he learned to read by age four—and oral histories, telling him stories of plantation life—stories he would retell in his poems, the first one written when he was only six.

After the divorce, Matilda devoted herself to stewarding Paul's education. She bought him novels and Civil War histories. By the time he was seven, she had installed a study in his room. At a time when most Daytonians, black and white, ended their education at eighth grade, she enrolled Paul in high school. When he entered Dayton Central High in 1886, he was the only African American in his class. The Wright brothers were his classmates, and they became lifelong friends and collaborators. Paul was popular at Central, and became the president of the schools' literary organization and editor of the paper. At sixteen, Paul published two poems in the highly selective *Dayton Herald*.

Central offered Dunbar a nondiscriminatory, nurturing education. But after graduating, he learned Central was the exception. No one would hire him. He ended up taking a job as an elevator operator in one of Dayton's major business buildings, earning four dollars a week. While riding up and down he read and wrote. He was the only elevator boy in Dayton "who had Homer, Virgil, Shakespeare, and Keats underneath his stool," Sci tells us. And he listened closely to his passengers. "If he heard a word he hadn't heard before he would look it up. He would listen to the speech forms," Sci says.

Dunbar also published poems while working his elevator job. In 1892, he was invited to give a reading at the Western Association of Writers' meeting in Dayton and was the first African American ever to be so honored. There, he met James Whitcomb Riley, then one of America's preeminent poets, known for his Midwestern dialect poems. Riley encouraged Dunbar to self-publish his first book of poetry, *Oak and Ivy,* in 1893. Dunbar sold it for one dollar, hawking it to his elevator passengers. The book was well reviewed, and Dunbar's name started to spread. He traveled the Midwest giving readings. In 1893, he went to Chicago to look for work at the World's Columbian Exposition. There, he met Frederick Douglass, then an elder statesman. Douglass hired him to help with his Haitian Exhibit.

Dunbar was successful in Chicago—he met prominent blacks and whites who supported his work. But, when he returned to Dayton after the fair, he once again found himself broke. In 1898, Dunbar had married Alice Ruth Moore, a college-educated, light-skinned New Orleanian, and they moved to Washington, D.C., bringing Matilda with him. Dunbar got a job at the Library of Congress, but it was tedious, and the dust in the stacks worsened his incipient case of tuberculosis. He quit, but his health declined.

By the time Dunbar landed in Washington, he had published *Majors and Minors*. The leading literary critic of the day, William Dean Howells, praised it in *Harper's Weekly*. Howells's review gave Dunbar the break he needed. Howells wrote that Dunbar was "the only man of pure African blood and of American civilization to feel the Negro life aesthetically and express it lyrically." Howells praised Dunbar's dialect poems, which he said "are really not dialect so much as delightful personal attempts and failures of the spoken language."

Paul Dunbar's success was always ambivalent, though. Howells's rave was tinged with racism. Dunbar wrote many conventional lyrics, but his use of dialect was his claim to fame and his albatross. Many critiqued him for stereotyping blacks.

But, as Sci points out, Dunbar didn't write in one dialect—he wrote in fourteen. He wrote in white dialects, and in dialects from all the southern states. White writers, such as Riley, Mark Twain, and Thomas Nelson Page, were gaining kudos for their dialect writing. But Dunbar suffered for his mimicry. He was called "the prince of the coon song writers." He grew to regret his use of dialect. Debates over his dialect poetry overshadowed the rest of his writing: everything from his traditionally formal poems, his novels, and his plays to his operas and even his newspaper editorials decrying racism. "I didn't start as a dialect poet. I simply came to the conclusion that I could write it as well, if not better, than anybody else I knew of, and that by doing so I should gain a hearing, . . . and now they don't want me to write anything but dialect," he told James Weldon Johnson.

In 1902, Dunbar left Washington and his wife, Alice. What started as an intense love affair ended, suddenly, four years later. Paul decided to move back to Dayton with Matilda.

Multiculturalism and identity politics are fairly new terms, but the struggle between assimilation and segregation has a long history in America. Paul Laurence Dunbar fought it during his tragically short life. His story, better than any, raises the difficult question of how much we should, or should not, read with an eye toward the race, gender or ethnicity of a writer.

Today, the author's face, race, sex, upbringing, and class all figure prominently in the buying and selling of literature, in how a book is marketed and, thus, how a reader engages with the book. Unfortunately, this embrace of emphasis on the biography and identity of the author can serve as a further ghettoizing of literature, as it did for Dunbar when he was alive.

A house museum is a handy symbol for the importance of biography and history to understanding literary text—to see the house is to understand the literature. There are risks, though. If the fit between the author and his history—or biography—is too perfect, then the house becomes a cage, and the author, a bird.

Paul lived in the Italianate brick house for two years. He set up Matilda with electricity, running water and a gas stove. The Dunbars were one of the few families in town with a telephone. One of the hardest things about explaining a historic house is contextualizing its class status at the time the writer lived in it. Though it may not seem like it anymore, the Dunbar House was well appointed for its time. Paul bought it after he had achieved success—and some money.

On the day Paul died, Matilda closed the door to Paul's study. She never let anyone inside for the thirty years she lived in the house afterward. She received many visitors in those decades, including Paul Robeson. Sometimes they brought her money, and sat with her at the ornate dining room table, which today is elaborately laid out for four. All the dishes and all the furnishings throughout the house are original, down, hauntingly, to Paul's toothbrush and mug in the upstairs bathroom, and Matilda's needle and thread. Paul's funeral flowers are still in the house, and they were the first things Matilda looked at in the morning and last thing at night.

In her will, Matilda left directions for how to preserve Paul's effects. She was, as Sci puts it, "the first person to conceive of memorializing her son," the first site manager, the first tour guide, the first woman to take it upon herself to passionately advocate for Dunbar's legacy.

So Paul's bedroom looks exactly as it did in 1906. It is not reconstructed, not set up "as if he were living here today." Sci shows us the daybed he died upon, his Central High School diploma, his Remington typewriter. He spent his last days here very depressed. " 'Why did I have to pioneer this experience?' he must have wondered," Sci muses. But, she reminds us, "he penned his compensation."

At the end of the tour, Sci asks us to sit in the chairs against the walls in the front entry room. She is about to send us back out into present-day Dayton, on a cold gray October day that has only grown bleaker during the time our small cohort has spent transfixed by her performance. In the dank entry room Sci leads us in another incantation.

"He was only singing. He sang of the human experience. Don't think he fell short of anything. Paul pioneered a new direction. Now, let's sing."

She has us recite the poem whose text we read when we entered the house, engraved on a faded plaque erected by Boy Scout Troop 30 in 1921. It sits on the front lawn, and consists solely of lines from "Compensation." This time she has us repeat each line after her.

"Because I had loved"
Because I had loved
"So deeply"
So deeply
"Because I had loved so long"
Because I had loved so long
"God in his great compassion"
God in his great compassion
"Gave me a gift of song."
Gave me a gift of song.

This time we get it right the first time.

I love the Paul Laurence Dunbar House in Dayton, Ohio. I love it because it is full of just the longing that I am seeking in these small museums. It was preserved by his mother in a stubborn, lonely vigil to have her son's reputation restored—so he would get one of those callbacks that Henry Louis Gates, Jr., talks about. Mother Dunbar outlived her son by three decades, an unimaginable length of time to a mother. I can trace a direct line from the house to Matilda Dunbar, ex-slave, through R.R. Gilbert and Sci. Because of this and because so few visit the house, because literary history has not been kind to Dunbar nor history to Dayton—for all these reasons I want to praise Dunbar, extol his house, sing his songs.

Poe Cottage, the Bronx

Chapter 9

Poe Houses and Arrested Decay

SAVANNAH, GEORGIA, IS KNOWN for its historic homes, particularly since John Berendt's novel *Midnight in the Garden of Good and Evil* helped bring them alive. Now you can visit Savannah for a weekend and tour gorgeous houses and squares, walk through well-appointed dining rooms admiring wallpaper choices, and hear tour guides explain the glamorous lives of wealthy former residents. It is a fine way to spend a few culture- and history-tinged days.

To house such tourists there are dozens of lovely bed and breakfasts to choose from, and they are their own subset of historical house, too, of course. So, you can sleep in a historic house in the Historic Quarter on your expedition to more historic houses. I stayed at the President's Quarter, opulent and comfortable, with a charming patio, wrought iron chairs, and fancy scrambled eggs.

But I did not visit the Mansion of Forsyth Park, or the Juliette Gordon Low Home. I did not take the Old Savannah Tour of "Pioneers in Preservation" or see the chandeliers in the Davenport House. I went to visit a Depression-era house lived in by a family that was barely middle class, a house that has also been restored to be historically accurate—which in this case is to say bland and bare-boned. It was hard to find and it is only open a few hours a day. The day I went I was the only visitor.

By the time I got to the Flannery O'Connor house in Savannah, I had had my fill of writers' houses. I was bored at looking at bedrooms, parlors, and writing desks, to be honest. Bill Dawers started to tell me how very excited he was about all the big plans for Flannery O'Connor House: they were going to expand hours, hire a part-time staff member, and start a book group. There is another O'Connor house, Andalusia, on the site of her farm in Milledgeville, Georgia, that is also open to the public, and the two houses work together to raise funds. I nodded as he spoke and put a smile on my face, but to myself I thought—no way. Their numbers will never rise as high as they hope.

In 1989, Savannah, before *Midnight in the Garden of Good and Evil* and the expansion of the Savannah College of Art and Design, was an aging town, not the sparkly, historic one it has become. A couple of English professors noted that Flannery O'Connor's childhood house was up for sale for $132,000. They bought it, formed a nonprofit, and opened the house to visitors on weekends. They ran it themselves, and keeping the place going was difficult. At times they considered closing the house to visitors. But with the help of a few volunteers they kept it open, and over the years they renovated, added rooms to the tour, and expanded their hours to six afternoons a week. They started selling books, mugs, and t-shirts. When I visited in fall of 2008, they were receiving about five visitors a day, and had just hired their first employee, a part-time assistant who lived in the apartment upstairs.

The economics of writers' houses are not very good. Nor, of course, are the economics of many writers, so perhaps it is fitting. Few owners of the houses decide to create an institution to mimic the writers' own economic woes, but ironically that is what often happens. The longest and most brutal test case of authorial poverty that presages writer's house financial woes is that of the Edgar Allan Poe houses.

Edgar Allan Poe moved a lot, almost always not by choice and out of economic necessity. Poe never owned a house: he rented. But after his death, many of his houses were bought precisely because of their association with Poe. The houses that he was forced out of became museums in his honor. There are four Poe museums scattered along the mid-Atlantic seaboard in the Bronx, Philadelphia, Baltimore, and Richmond. (Poe never lived in the house in Richmond that is now the Edgar Allan Poe Museum, though you can visit his restored dorm room at the University of Virginia.)

Since Poe left few possessions, none contain much in the way of authentic furnishings. One, the Edgar Poe House in Philadelphia, is preserved according to the historic preservation principle called "arrested decay," in which structures are maintained only to the extent that they will not fall over or deteriorate in similarly extreme ways. It is a good phrase for any Poe House. The houses remain small. Oddly, given the enormous demographic changes that have occurred in the last century and a half, they are all in what are now poor neighborhoods. Taken together, the three form a map of restless underachievement. Poe may take top honors for most writers' houses, but it is a dubious distinction.

He was canonized early, which explains the number of museums. But during his lifetime, he was not nearly so popular. Often drunk, irascible, and harshly critical of his peers, Poe had many enemies. Many considered his lifestyle too corrupt for his literature to be ennobling or worthwhile. He could never make ends meet as a writer. Far more money has been thrown at him since his death than he ever made.

The Bronx Poe house is a small, white cottage, and I could not help but notice the similarities between it and my house in Oberlin that was then languishing on the market. Both Poe's and mine are farmhouses, with wide plank flooring, small windows, and a large porch for sitting and rocking. They belong in the middle of fields, obviously, and that is where mine sits. But the Poe Cottage is in the middle of a traffic median. Confused drivers trying to change lanes ceaselessly circle around it. It is, ironically, the only writer's house museum in New York City.

One cannot help but laugh—and then cough from the fumes, while you stand on the porch—when you learn that Poe moved into this 1812 house for the air. In 1846, Poe was living with his wife, Virginia, in Manhattan. Virginia had tuberculosis, so they moved uptown for healthier air. Poe had just received acclaim for "The Raven," but he was still broke. He paid $100 a month for the house anyway, hoping to save Virginia. The gamble failed and she died in the tiny bedroom on the first floor a year after they moved in. Poe stayed there for two more. When he was famously found dead in the streets of Baltimore in 1849, it was still his home.

The New York Shakespeare Society saved the house from demolition in 1895. The state wanted to widen Kingsbridge Road and demolish the house, but the group lobbied to have the cottage moved instead. It was one of the first acts of historic preservation on behalf of a literary house in America. A speech by the society's president, Appleton Morgan, appeals to nationalism as a way to encourage support of the house's preservation:

> I think we should hang our heads for our country and for ourselves, when we think that while for half a century we have, as a nation, contributed liberally to every appeal to build memorials to the poets and the writers of other nations; while we have aided to erect deserved monuments to Shelley, to Keats, to Tennyson, even to Carlyle, who growled and bit his nails at us, we have utterly neglected and ignored the grandest and most unique, the most noble, and the sweetest of our own poets. . . . We have utterly and shamefully neglected our brother, who, if we have one at all, was and is certainly our American Shakespeare.

Morgan's words were effective. The society managed to save the house and built Poe Park around it. In 1909, the Bronx Society of Arts and Sciences installed a bronze bust of Poe in the park to commemorate the centennial of his birth. It was vandalized, and eventually brought inside the house, where you can still find it today. In 1913, the house was moved 450 feet to where it now stands.

By the time the house was moved, the Bronx was no longer rural. Poe Park became a community center, and stood handsomely as a backdrop for bandleaders like Jimmy Dorsey, Benny Goodman, and Glenn Miller who held concerts there. But the house was not maintained and fell into disrepair. It wasn't until the 1970s that it was taken over by the Bronx County Historical Society. As with the statue, vandals damaged the house itself. To prevent further decay, the society hired a caretaker to live in the house. It is a lonely job to be sure, to live in that almost two-hundred-year-old farm-house, where Poe's wife died, and where very few tourists enter. That may well change, if all goes according to plan. In July 2008, the house shut down for repairs. It was renovated, and a $4.2 million visitor center designed by architect Toshiko Mori was added next door. The center is shaped like a raven's wing.

There was no one else there the day I went. Like my farmhouse, not many show up to see the inside. The caretaker was a seventh-grade teacher who said she took the job because she likes talking to people. She was excited to give a tour to my friend and me. There is little inside the house, and everything felt very close. I went outside, to the park, and looked at the bodegas and pawnshops through the prism of the cars driving the four-lane road between the park and the commercial stretch across from it. My friend emerged from the house smiling and happy. She had more patience than I with the tour guide's eager patter. For me, the Poe Cottage was almost too incongruous to bear, too jarring, too out of place.

It is very near Little Albania, and I was excited to go visit. Little Albania is exotic in that way that off-the-beaten track places are supposed to be in the Bronx. Kosovo had declared independence the day earlier, and everyone was in a festive mood, sporting Kosovar t-shirts and waving little Albanian flags that were for sale in every storefront. I ate delicious things I had never heard of for lunch. My friend and I laughed a lot. Despite the hard and important work of the Bronx County Historical Society, for now, Little Albania beats out an old farmhouse sitting in the middle of a traffic median for recommended cool things to do in the Bronx.

The Poe house in Philadelphia is preserved as a ruin. The idea behind "arrested decay" is to prevent visitors from making false connections in their mind between what was original to the house and what is not. If the desk that Poe wrote on does not exist, they do not put in another desk from the same era—or "conjectural period pieces." As the museum's cura-tor Mary Jenkins put it, "It would be too easy for visitors to assume and remember them as Poe's own furniture."

It is, of course, common to consider authors' houses haunted, and Poe houses most of all. But if the Philadelphia house is haunted, it is with unlikely and thus charming contentedness. The National Park Service runs this house, and it is the best operated and most historically appropriate of the Poe houses. Poe lived in Philadelphia for six years, but in this house on

North Seventh Street for only one or two. He was productive and fairly happy in the house, able to walk from his home to the publishing houses about one mile away. Since he rented the house, and no one knows how it was furnished, or where the furnishings are today, there is not much inside the rooms. Like those in the Bronx, they are mainly bare and cold.

The house is on a corner of busy and charmless stretch of Spring Garden Street, on the borders between Old City with its art galleries, restaurants, and condominiums, the ever-gentrifying neighborhood of Northern Liberties, and the ever-struggling neighborhoods of North Philadelphia. The volunteers at the house caution visitors not to explore the neighborhoods to the north. The house is also surrounded by public housing, brick, tall, and thin, like the Poe house. When I visited, I attended a historical reenactment of a lecture by Helen Whitman, who was briefly engaged to Poe at the end of his life. A woman in a huge purple crinoline dress spoke to a dozen or so others in a small auditorium in the house. It was a sparkling spring day, and it was hard to sit in that cold and dark room and hear a melodramatic one-woman performance—suited to the time, of course, and the actress's mastery of her speech was impressive. Still, I could hear a man outside announcing through a microphone that he had produce for sale, which made me daydream about people going out from their apartments into the sun to buy carrots from his truck.

The house is very much geared to entertaining children, and you can earn a junior park ranger badge by doing activities with items placed inside a travel trunk. Children are encouraged to imagine similarities between themselves and long-ago people and times. For instance, when you enter the parlor, the guide tells you: "A friend visited Eddie here. He recalled being served a delicious dish of 'peaches in the melting mood.' . . . *If you were entertaining your friends here, what kind of dessert would you serve?*" It is a very smart, creative way to engage in history without anachronism, a problem that many writers' houses, and visitors, trip over again and again.

The Poe House in Baltimore is the house best associated with the popular image of Poe we enjoy today—the creepy master of spooky stories who was found dead of unknown circumstances on election day. It is also the one that most forces any visitor to confront the present when seeking out the past.

An episode of the television series *The Wire*, set in the same West Baltimore neighborhood where Poe's house is located, begins with a white tourist asking some guys on a stoop where he can find the Poe House. "Poe house? Look around you, every house 'round here is a po' house," they answer.

The day I visited the West Baltimore Poe House on 203 Amity Street I was that white lady, driving around the streets in a rental car, slowing down to check for street names. The first time I drove by the house—which is open from noon to three Thursdays, Fridays, and Saturdays—I saw a paper taped to the door announcing that it had been "closed for emergency." It was a Friday. I had flown to Baltimore for one day to see the house and was sick thinking it might be closed on Saturday, too.

When I returned, after a brief detour to hang out in a grocery store parking lot filled with cop cars, the house had reopened. On the corner by the house was an old-timey lamppost. Across the street was an overgrown, abandoned lot surrounded by vacant row houses with "No Trespassing" sprayed in red on boards covering windows and doors. A cop in a patrol car was stationed nearby.

The "closed" sign was now gone, revealing the permanent sign behind it. This one asked visitors not to give admission money until they got inside the house. It also requested that visitors not encourage panhandlers and that they refuse any solicitations.

I rang the bell, and Jeff Jerome, the sole employee, opened the door. "Please stand over there," he said, gesturing to the other side of the very small entry room. One institutional-looking chair sat by the wall. I stood next to it. Jerome asked the mother and son who had joined me outside, waiting for the house to open, if they would like to come in. They replied that they were still waiting for a friend, so he advised them to stay outside until she arrived. Then Jerome quickly closed the door and immediately launched into a well-rehearsed standard welcome spiel. It was a self-guided tour, he told me, and the brochure—copies of which were hanging on a nearby wall—had information I could read as I wandered through the house. There was a video on the second floor, he continued, that ranged in quality from good to poor—so, he asked of me, please do not come down and tell him something's wrong with the videotape, because he knows that already, and there's nothing that can be done to improve the quality.

I paid my nominal admission fee and wandered about the tiny five-room house Poe lived in with about five other family members from 1832 to 1835. While residing in the house Poe wrote "MS Found in a Bottle," which won him a $50 prize from a Baltimore newspaper for best short story. He also married Virginia here. But in 1835, his grandmother died, and since she had been paying the rent through her pension, the family had to move.

When the house was built, the location, like that of the Bronx cottage, was still quaintly pastoral. The house was almost torn down in 1941 so that the city could build the ironically named Poe Homes, a public housing project. But members of the Edgar Allan Poe Society forced the local housing authority to spare the site. In 1949, the Poe Society opened the house as a museum, and they ran it until the city took it over in the late 1970s.

Jerome has been the house museum's only employee since the day it reopened in 1979. Before he became the curator, Jerome was hired as a photographer to shoot the Poe grave. Jerome has been a Poe buff ever since he was twelve. He snuck into a theater to see the Vincent Price movie *Tales of Terror*, which was rated four bloody Xs, which meant no one under thirteen would be admitted. The movie led to his lifelong fascination with Poe. When the city decided to make the house a monument, he was the natural choice to run it.

Jerome wrote the text for the fact sheet given to visitors. Just reading it gives you a sense of the place:

Why does the Poe House have that "old" house smell?

The Poe House is an old house and with the age comes the tell tale odor which only an old house has. Even with limited air conditioning this odor will appear and then vanish. It is most noticeable after it has been raining.

Is the house haunted?

Some people have strong feelings about "ghosts" and other related subjects. They are deeply offended by these claims due to religious beliefs. A historic site that claims to have had "ghostly" events also stands the chance of being accused of making up stories to bolster attendance. For these and other reasons the Poe House has a policy of not discussing supernatural events that may or may not have occurred during its past history. Any soft whispering that you may hear coming from no visible source is your imagination.

What spooked me about the house was not this fear but the strong echo of poverty: the poverty of the Poe family when they lived here, and the poverty of the neighborhood today.

I started exploring. I was tentative about where I tread, given the sign in the first display room. Under a glass display box sitting in the middle of the room was a sign that read: "CAUTION. Historic homes are fragile . . . The Poe House was not constructed for tourism . . . All the windows are off centered. Some are lopsided while others are recessed into the wall. Two rooms have floor's [*sic*] that are not level. Don't let your kids run around."

On the second floor was a small room with peeling plaster, an old lamp in the corner, and a window air conditioner held in place by cardboard. A dozen or so brown folding chairs were lined up against a wall. In the front of them was an old, faux-wood TV stand with a television that played the video Jerome had warned me about. The video was on a loop, and a fading sign told me the tape would automatically stop playing at three o'clock. The video presentation contained clips from local Baltimore news broadcasts, assorted short sixty- or ninety-second pieces about the Poe House, the Poe grave, and the city's Halloween celebration. The film quality, as Jerome warned, was very poor: static-filled and crackly and snowy. The anchors sported mid-1980s hairstyles. Jerome was featured in most of the clips. I found myself transfixed by the grainy images of feathered hair. I thought a lot about TV news of 1980s, well before the advent of the Internet, and about the culture of local 5 P.M. broadcasts.

One of the clips in the loop was from the Bronx Poe house. By the second frame you knew it was "educational," the kind of thing that would have been, in an earlier age, a filmstrip shown to elementary school kids. The title shot told me it was part of the "Bronx County Faces and Places" series. It opened with three kids standing on a street corner. They talk about how they have to choose a topic for a report on a famous person who lived in the Bronx. "George Washington or Poe, who should we choose?" they ask before having a stilted, scripted debate on the merits of each. I imagined them practicing their lines at recess. "Edgar Allan Poe invented the horror story," says one kid. "He's like Stephen King. People being buried alive and stuff." Another child actor adds that he also invented the detective story: "Like *Moonlighting*. Where would *Moonlighting* be without him?"

While my mind was happily pondering this question, the kids on screen joined their classmates for a field trip to the Edgar Allan Poe house. While most of them head into one room, the boy who was advocating Stephen King–like Poe as the subject of his report hears a book fall on the floor. He starts reading it, and then—cue eerie music—a rocking chair begins to rock *all by itself!* He hears a voice that sounds a bit like Vincent Price, reading aloud the very words the boy had been reading in the book. Then, Edgar Allan Poe himself appears! He talks to the boy about how Washington is an inferior, not really Bronx-type choice for a report, and how when he lived in the house, the Bronx was still the countryside.

"The countryside? How could that be?!" the boy responds with that wonderfully studied air. "There aren't any fields here! This is the Bronx. There are buildings everywhere."

Poe sighs and laments that now you can only hear the "coughing of automobiles."

I got up from the moldy video room and climbed a set of tiny stairs and then up another, even tinier set of stairs, to the attic room. You cannot enter the room, as it is roped off, but you can look up from the stairwell at the underside of a bed frame and a table. There is something furtive about peeking your head from the stairs to the bottom of someone's bed. I descended, slightly dizzy, and found Jerome. I congratulated him on a recent *New York Times* article that featured him. While we chatted, people rang the bell. He stopped talking to me, opened the door and asked them to stand on the other side of the room. Then he closed the door and gave them the exact same spiel he'd given me just minutes earlier. A typical Saturday sees about 50 visitors; roughly 5,000 people tour the house each year.

As I hung out in the small entry room, which also doubles as Jerome's workspace, an elderly man came in, breathless and sweating. It was a muggy and hot day in Baltimore—well into the nineties. The man, who I imagined to be a World War II vet, wore a khaki shirt and pants, a fanny pack around his waist, and a stiff baseball cap that sat high on his head. His armpits had huge sweat stains on them. He sat in the folding chair in the lobby to catch his breath.

"I took the bus and got off when I saw the E. A. Poe sign on the street, but it's a long walk from the bus," the man said.

"Well, those signs are for cars driving by, not walkers," Jerome explained. "If you go to the website we let you know that."

The man sat, catching his breath. "I wake up dreaming about Edgar Allan Poe," he said to neither of us in particular. "Sometimes he comes to me as I go about my day. And that old-time actor, what's his name?"

"Vincent Price?" Jerome said.

"Yes, Vincent Price," he responded. Then he pointed to a portrait on the wall. "That must be the sister, huh?"

"No, it's not. You can read the text below it," Jerome stated.

Jerome then turned to me to continue our discussion of the *New York Times* article, which featured a mock debate he had with a scholar in Philadelphia who believes Poe's remains should be returned to that city. The pair used this staged argument to publicize an upcoming bicentennial celebration in Philadelphia at which Jerome would be speaking. "There's nothing more boring than a meeting of the Edgar Allan Poe Society. Have you ever been to one? Yawn," he said. "They spend all this time discussing the placement of a comma. I mean, I know there's a place for all that, but if I'm going to those meetings, I'm going to be entertaining. That's how we came up with the idea of the war. If I'm going to go to these talks, I'm going to at least make it fun for people. By having this war, we will also inform them about Poe. I'm going to bring a body bag, shovel, and rope with me. I'm going to put them on the table and say: you want to snatch a body? Go ahead. Do you know what we do with body snatchers in Baltimore? We hang them."

The Poe houses map contemporary American urban poverty, East Coast style, from the Bronx to Philadelphia to West Baltimore. Because of their connection to Poe, houses that otherwise would have fallen apart are preserved and open to tourists. Like visiting the Whitman house in Camden, visiting the Poe houses takes us to neighborhoods we might otherwise skip.

All three are run by civic institutions—the federal government, a county, and a city—that never have enough money. Nor did Poe, always broke, never able to own a house, or stay in a rented house for long. We could have restored other Poe houses—he lived in many. Does the presence of all these houses signal his success as an American author or failure? And are these museums indicators of America's economic growth and expansion since Poe's death in 1849, or sure proof of our failures to better conditions for all those in need?

We see this double display of poverty—that of the author then, and that of the town now, at houses other than the Poe ones: in Camden, Dayton, and Hannibal, and in Pittsfield, Massachusetts. In 1850 Herman Melville (1819–1892) bought a house in Pittsfield called Arrowhead—a Georgian style farmhouse built in 1780. The Melvilles were crowded inside—between 1850 and 1863, Melville lived there with his wife, four children, his mother, and three aunts. To create space, he added to the house as he added to his oeuvre. "I have been building some shanties of houses (connected with the old ones) and likewise some shanties of chapters and essays," he once wrote to Nathaniel Hawthorne of his ramshackle additions. Many visitors are surprised by how small Arrowhead is, and how little Melville earned from his writing—only $10,000 his entire life. Those relatively small figures, however, are part of the curatorial lesson of the house: "Melville never made his fortune here, but you get to see what it was like to be a working writer," one tour guide put it. "I want people to see the conditions he worked under, to understand the pressures he felt. I want them to see his dedication."

I was wrong about the Flannery O'Connor house. It has done pretty well. In early 2009, a major new biography of O'Connor by Brad Gooch was published to many praising reviews. The biography led to an uptick in O'Connor interest, and visitors. When Gooch came to the house to launch his book, three hundred people showed up, and many bought copies donated by the publisher. Since then, average weekend numbers of visitors have doubled. These days, Dawers says, they net about nine dollars per visitor—five for admission, and the rest in product sales. And the house, worth $132,000 twenty years ago, is now worth much more, given the boom in Savannah's real estate market. Dawers, a tireless promoter, has started a Facebook fan club and a book group.

The O'Connor house is privately owned and has benefitted from Savannah becoming a tourist-friendly spot. That explains their success, modest though it is. One could mark American demographic changes by the houses that are doing well, traffic-wise. Not the ones in the Rust Belt, but Jack London's house in California is thriving, as is O'Connor's. That was not the case when the authors were alive, of course: Glen Ellen and Savannah were far less glamorous then than they are now.

What remains constant are impoverished American cities. A visit to the Poe houses, particularly the one in Baltimore near the Poe Houses public housing project, drives that point home, again and again and again.

Where Charles Chesnutt once lived

Chapter 10

At Home with Charles Chesnutt
and Langston Hughes

THERE ARE NO WRITERS' HOUSE MUSEUMS in Cleveland, where I now live. In the past year, I have discovered the former houses of two writers, though. These houses put me to the test: did I wish they were museums?

Charles Chesnutt made the city his home for decades, and was a prominent figure in town. Although Chesnutt is little known today to most Americans, his reputation is quite high among American literature scholars. I was assigned his work in graduate school and was incredulous that I had not heard of his proto-modernist novels of race relations in the Reconstruction South, nor of his dialect-based stories of plantation life. In his day, Chesnutt was celebrated. Then he fell off the literary map.

Chesnutt, the quintessential American self-made man, was born in Cleveland in 1858 to parents who, as free blacks from North Carolina, had moved north before the Civil War. After the war, the family moved back to North Carolina, where Charles lived from ages eight to twenty-six. Although he had little formal education, he taught himself German, Latin, history, literature, and law, and became a teacher and school principal.

Chesnutt, who could pass for white, felt out of place in the South, where his skin color, background, and education made him feel "neither fish, flesh nor fowl." He returned North, settling in Cleveland with his wife and children. In Cleveland, he passed the Ohio bar exam with the highest scores in his test-taking class and established a successful legal stenography business. But his ambition was to become a professional author. As he wrote in his journal at the age of twenty, he wanted to write to accomplish political purposes: "The object of my writing would not be so much the elevation of the colored people as the elevation of the whites—for I consider the unjust spirit of caste . . . so insidious as to pervade a whole nation. . . . I consider this a barrier to the moral progress of the American people: and I would be one of the first to head a determined, organized crusade against it."

He achieved his dream. He was the first African American to publish a story in the preeminent literary magazine of the day, the *Atlantic Monthly*. The magazine's reputation-making editor, William Dean Howells, compared Chesnutt to Henry James, Guy de Maupassant, and Ivan Turgenev. Chesnutt's literary career was launched.

After these early successes, Chesnutt turned to his most ambitious project, *The Marrow of Tradition*, published in 1901, a novel based on the Wilmington race riots of 1898. He conceived his magnum opus as a successor to *Uncle Tom's Cabin*. *Marrow* portrays a sweeping range of southern characters, conditions, and race relations. But the white readers he aimed to elevate through aesthetic and moral suasion were not ready for this most harrowing indictment of racism. After reading the novel, Howells, once his champion, wondered, "How he must hate us."

Marrow did not sell well, and Chesnutt, no longer able support himself as a writer, returned to the law. He remained socially and politically active, though, and, along with Booker T. Washington and W. E. B. Du Bois, championed better treatment of blacks in the South and advocated for blacks in Cleveland. In 1928, he was awarded the Spingarn Medal by the NAACP for his "pioneer work as a literary artist depicting the life and struggle of Americans of Negro descent, and for his long and useful career as scholar, worker, and freeman of one of America's greatest cities."

In 1889 he had settled in a nice house in a comfortable neighborhood. During a phenomenally productive six-year period, he wrote seven novels and many articles and short stories in that house.

I did some research at the public library. I discovered that Chesnutt lived in two houses in Cleveland neighborhoods that were then, at the beginning of the twentieth century, middle class and integrated. I did not expect his blocks to be well appointed any more. The area has not been middle class for decades; it has been poor, forlorn, and forgotten for some time. And with the housing downturn, the foreclosures had skyrocketed in the area. Abandoned houses, I imagined, would outnumber lived-in ones.

It took me just a few minutes of searching online to find the addresses, thanks to the Cleveland Public Library's Digital Archives, and I learned from the Archives that the house that he lived in for almost thirty years after he had stopped writing was torn down years ago when a school was built. The other house was where Chesnutt wrote obsessively and prolifically. The Cleveland Public Library Digital Archives listed that one as being at 64 Brenton Avenue, which today is 2212 East 73rd Street.

I drove to 73rd Street to find Chesnutt's house—it took me eight minutes to get there from the house I had just moved into. I thought I would maybe knock on the door and ask the current resident if he knew a famous writer once lived there. I did not find the house. But on that block I found something even more inspiring.

It was a brilliant, seventy-degree, sunny day—a rarity in November in Cleveland. When I turned onto 73rd Street and saw a row of boarded-up brick duplexes with "No Copper Stay Out" spray-painted on the doors, I was not shocked. What I saw next did surprise me, though.

Three newly built, vinyl-sided houses lined the block past the boarded-up ones. They sat primly, mums blooming in front. The grass was freshly mowed, and the autumn leaves were a glorious yellow. Across the street was another typically American scene, a pretty house with Halloween decorations out front.

I kept driving slowly up the block. I passed lots filled with grass and more sparkling-leaved trees. The empty spaces filled with plant life give the block an oddly bucolic feel. I found a few more abandoned houses, too, but they had been carefully boarded up. Something unusual was happening on East 73rd Street.

I was driving very slowly, and the mailman peered in my car curiously. White ladies in Volkswagens are not typical on this block. I waved at the mailman and continued my crawl. I was squinting to find house numbers. I found 2216. I found 2208. I backed up. 2212 should have been between those two houses. But there was no 2212. There was, instead, a driveway, blocked off with a locked fence, and behind it, a garage.

A man was on the other side of the fence, pacing about. His dogs were running around the driveway. I pulled over and rolled down the window.

"Excuse me, sir," I said. "Which house is 2212?"

"There is no 2212," he replied. "Right here," he said, pointing down to the concrete driveway, "is where 2212 was. It was torn down about twelve years ago." I turned off the engine.

George Tuggle, the man I met, is handsome, strong, and tall. He sported a mustache, a western hat, a gray cotton shirt tucked into jeans, and boots. He had a drawl I later learned was Georgian. He was happy to help me with my obscure research quest. Tuggle owns all three lots. They have been in his family since the 1940s, when his uncle moved north. Tuggle's porch is charmingly festooned with whirligigs—he is a master woodworker. In the electrical pole in front of his driveway is a "DRUG FREE ZONE" sign.

Tuggle had never heard of Chesnutt. When the house was taken down for the driveway, no one remembered Chesnutt used to live in it. I asked about the new houses, the boarded-up ones, the lots.

"Well, the block group is very active," he told me. Tuggle and other residents of East 73rd, tired of the empty houses being squatted in by drug dealers and prostitutes, lobbied the city council for a year and a half to remove the five gigantic abandoned houses. Finally, in August 2008, the planning commissioner came by, and agreed to take them down within thirty days. The block group did not believe him, and promised to have a demolition party if he made good. He did, and the party was attended by the mayor and other public officials.

Weed and Seed, a federally funded community program, support the block group. Their presence in the neighborhood is due to hard work by Burten, Bell, Carr, a community development corporation for ward 5. Burten, Bell, Carr is also responsible for the new houses, part of their East Central Project. East 73rd Street was a marquee street for the project because it had been so beset by problems, and because the residents were active. All the new houses on the block, completed in 2006, are still owned by the original buyers.

After I returned home, I called Burten, Bell, Carr and asked if they knew anything about Chesnutt and his house. It was all news to them. I made an appointment to go meet with them. We sat in their swanky new office near E. 73rd Street. I told them what I knew about Chesnutt, and they told me what they knew about George Tuggle and the E. 73rd block group. Then we got to talking about how we might honor Chesnutt's legacy on the block, something that might also honor the work of the dedicated residents of East 73rd Street today, Tuggle and his neighbors, who have done so much to improve the block.

What about those abandoned lots? I asked. What are they thinking of doing with those? "They are talking about a community garden," said executive director Timothy Tramble.

Is it a loss not to preserve this lot as a museum to Chesnutt? Many other writers lack a house museum. Say you want to see where Wallace Stevens wrote his poems. No luck. Say it is Isaac Bashevis Singer's apartment you would like to view. Well, you could look at the building from West 86th Street, and try to figure out which window was his. You cannot visit the houses of Ralph Ellison, Henry James, Theodore Dreiser, or Sylvia Plath. The list goes on.

Sometimes acts of nonpreservation are intentional, political or appropriate, as with the case of T. S. Eliot. Eliot grew up in Saint Louis, but he left the city "so early and so finally," as Eliot scholar David Chinitz puts it, that there has been bad blood between native son and tourist boosters ever since. "The enthusiasm from the community was sorely lacking," said Leslie Konnyu of an early effort to build a museum. "There was even outright opposition. Some write him off because he was an expatriate . . . others don't like the idea of his [early] negative poetry." Chinitz puts it clearly: "Since Eliot left the city as a 16-year-old and intentionally distanced himself from his Midwestern roots throughout his life, to the point of becoming a British citizen, it is not surprising that he's not the favorite native son; he also had to compete for that honor with the vastly more popular Samuel Clemens. He didn't recognize St. Louis; they don't recognize him . . . the relationship between the poet and his native country, let alone his native city, remains problematic."

The absence of a T. S. Eliot house museum then is fitting not only because of the bad blood between him and St. Louis, but also because Eliot himself did not believe in honoring writers' lives, at least according to his criticism. In "Tradition and the Individual Talent," Eliot argued, "The progress of an artist is a continual self-sacrifice, a continual extinction of personality." For Eliot, the poet (or writer of any kind) needs to absorb the history of poetry, not express his personality: "The poet has, not a 'personality' to express, but a particular medium." So too must the critic avoid the personal: "Honest criticism and sensitive appreciation is directed not upon the poet but upon the poetry . . . the poet is [not] in any way remarkable or interesting."

The lack of a museum does not mean less appreciation for Eliot, as his poetry is widely available. There is even a "Love Song to J. Alfred Prufrock" Wii virtual reality game, a fine alternative to a material house, and one that is arguably much more fun. Plus, the story of the Eliot nonhouse—like the stories of the Charles Chesnutt nonhouse—are as fascinating to research as are those of the extant houses. These lost houses are virtual ruins, one step removed from London's Wolf House. They provide me the same succor and sadness. They display the interconnections between physical and imaginary, past and present, fact and fiction—the vortex of issues that all real museums display.

I don't long for the nonhouses, because it is longing that I find at the houses that do exist. The absences make these places real to me, and sometimes presence only gets in my way. I prefer burnt stones and arrested decay to fake manuscripts on borrowed desks. I am grateful I was able to stand in the rather horrible living room where Hemingway killed himself, but I do not think it should become a museum, and thus I am uncomfortably sided with those greedy wealthy fourth-home owners in Ketchum who blocked it. As long as books are in print—or online or in ebooks—the authors remain accessible to all. If we want to do something more, there are certainly many deserving students and writers who would appreciate a fellowship, or scholarship, or even a residency in a writer's name. There is so little money in writing; there is not enough money to keep the houses that are open in the black. Why put more dollars into shoring up the domiciles of the literary past?

These conclusions have led me to conclude we need to restore no more houses in the memory of writers. And that made me feel very mean and uncharitable when I went to the Cleveland house that Langston Hughes once lived in. Pizza crusts, empty bags of spicy potato chips, and wrapping papers lay scattered over the green carpet. Huge holes dotted the walls where the fixtures had been ripped out. The back door was open. "People will spend all day trying to get ten cents worth of copper," Jay Gardner told me as he picked up an old grate and put it across the door latch to prevent another break-in. A week earlier, the Fairfax Renaissance Development Corporation had purchased the two-story house in Cleveland's Fairfax neighborhood after it had been foreclosed upon and sold at a sheriff's auction. It cost them $16,667. Gardner, community development officer for the corporation, is excited about the house's prospects. The corporation plans to spend $80,000–$100,000 to restore it to its original condition and have it designated as a historic landmark.

Hughes lived here for about two years, starting in 1917, while he was in high school. He had moved to Cleveland shortly before with his mother, and when she left town he moved into this house at 2266 East 86th Street. He rented out the attic room. "The only thing I knew how to cook myself in the kitchen of the house where I roomed was rice, which I boiled to a paste. Rice and hot dogs, rice and hot dogs, every night for dinner. Then I read myself to sleep." When the Fairfax group discovered the Hughes connection to the foreclosed house over the summer, they decided to buy the property. Dreaming big, they are considering selling the house to someone who would open it up as a museum. As we walk through the living room Gardner points out the original woodwork on the banisters and moldings.

When Hughes lived here the neighborhood housed assorted immigrants. Poles, Jews, Irish, Italians, and blacks resided side by side in houses pressed up close to each other on long blocks. Hughes attended Central High School, Cleveland's first and most prestigious public high school (also John D. Rockefeller's alma mater). One of the few black students, Hughes was a big man on campus: he starred on the track and field team and edited the literary magazine. In Cleveland, presumably in the attic rooms that are now empty and lime green, he began to write.

Then he left. If he attended university in the city, he would face dim prospects later, as opportunities for educated black men in Cleveland were thin. He was not from the city, anyway. He returned briefly in 1930 to participate in the premieres of his plays at Karamu House (then called Playhouse Settlement). By then, Fairfax had become overwhelmingly black.

As industry grew, so did the neighborhood: by the 1940s, it was home to 37,000 people.

Today it is home to 8,000. Most are older, low- to moderate-income African American couples whose kids have moved out. Some houses on East 86th Street are abandoned, while others are well maintained. This checkerboard pattern, created by the loss of industry and housing values, is a common sight in the city.

Fairfax Renaissance Development started a program to entice employees of the Cleveland Clinic and other nearby employers to buy property last year. The clinic is Cleveland's largest employer, and much of it lies in Fairfax. You can see one of the clinic's many shiny buildings from the porch of the Hughes house.

Not many have signed up for the housing program, according to Gardner, largely because the adjacent suburbs of Cleveland Heights and Shaker Heights are equally affordable. "Being a community developer in Cleveland is a little like being a Browns fan," Gardner says of the city's pathetic NFL team with irrationally optimistic fans. "We may be 1 and 9 but it's not so bad. Did you see that play last week?" he jokes. "Selling a neighborhood is like marketing a product. A city or a neighborhood is a store and you have to sell things people want to buy or people won't come. We don't have enough stuff to sell. We need to get people here, somehow." Gardner and I, done with our tour of the Hughes house, decide to grab some coffee. "Let's go to Cleveland Heights," he suggests, and we drive five minutes to a Starbucks.

Gardner thinks a Langston Hughes house museum might entice folks to Fairfax as well as help "tie folks to the legacy of the neighborhood." He is building a housing complex for grandparents raising grandchildren, and imagines a museum would be great for the kids who will live there.

Both the Fairfax neighborhood and American writers' house museums are snapshots of American demographic trends. There are dozens of house museums in New England, many in the mid-Atlantic and Midwest, and only a scattered few out west. Not surprisingly, our revered dead writers have lived in the areas of the country that drew immigrants to agricultural and then industrial jobs and are now hit hard by economic changes. Until a new wave of famous authors die—San Francisco 2100?—writers' house museums will continue to be clustered east of the Mississippi.

Even an attempt to establish a Langston Hughes museum in gentrified Harlem failed recently. It is not just those in depressed neighborhoods or cities that struggle, as the tourist-friendly and well-located O'Connor house in Savannah and Wharton house in the Berkshires attest.

Add to this the grim reality that in my city, as in many other cities that once housed now dead authors, housing is too much with us. As I drive around, I cannot help but wish we could find a way to neatly regroup the city into tighter blocks, as in a Tetris game, It seems so churlish, but I cannot get behind a Hughes museum fundraising campaign.

I asked Gardner if Hughes was a major figure among Fairfax residents. He said no, most of the name recognition stems from the Renaissance Corporation's own promotions of the writer's Cleveland connection and Hughes's connection to Karamu House. Why not redirect our energy to reading Hughes rather than restoring his house, I ask? His books are plentiful and inexpensive. It would not be cost prohibitive to give every resident of Fairfax a book, or every teacher a classroom set of, say, *Poetry for Young People*.

As I toured the house on East 86th Street, I thought of Hughes's lines about dreams deferred, which might "sag like a heavy load" and "stink like rotten meat." Or, of course, explode. There is no one answer to the woes of the rust belt, and yes, you can buy a house here for the same amount as a bathroom renovation in Manhattan. But cities go up and down—even London was more populous in 1931 than it is today. No matter how much we value our literary legacy, a writer's house will not give Fairfax the product placement it needs to sell more inventory.

It may be time to stop thinking of restoring houses as the keystone of either literary tourism or a strategy for reversing the depopulation of cities and to start building, as Emerson put it in "Circles," worlds: "Every spirit builds itself a house; and beyond its house, a world; and beyond its world a heaven. Know then, that the world exists for you: build, therefore, your own world." Hughes knew that, I suspect, huddled in that attic room eating rice and hot dogs. He knew that the world of the imagination would offer him more than the city, more than a house.

When I was a master's degree candidate in English, I spoke with the director of graduate admissions about my application for a Ph.D. program. She told me I should write my personal essay with care. "Do not," she told me, "tell me you want to get a Ph.D. because you '*loooove* literature,'" she said, pausing on the "o" in *love* for a long time to emphasize her mockery. We both laughed. I was in on the joke then. I knew that a passion for reading was not a good reason to get a Ph.D. Good reasons had to do with being engaged in literature's role in political change, or being intellectually attuned to the formal qualities of modernism, or committed to the project of ensuring that women and minority writers be included in the literary canon. It was hilarious to think someone would be so as naïve as to think "loving literature" would qualify you for admission to a Ph.D. program in English.

Now that I am a professor, students often come to me seeking advice about graduate school admissions. I often tell them the same thing I was told by years ago: just do not say you "loooove literature." But they never get the joke. They look at me surprised, confused. I used to take this as a sign they were not suited for graduate study. Now I regret that I mocked a passion for reading as a reason to commit to seven years of poverty and student loans in pursuit of an advanced degree.

To completely dismiss the emotional relationship a reader has with authors is to risk ending up cynical, as I was before I started visiting writers' houses. In the case of contemporary scholarly literary studies, it runs the risk of becoming marginal. The real naïveté lies in discounting a reader's relationship with the biography and background of an author.

My travels have led me to realize that despite being an English professor, I may not be the ideal reader of literary texts. They have also left me energized, too. I no longer feel I need to wall myself off from people who *loooove* literature. Nor do I find myself grumbling about how nobody outside academe reads anymore. I believe, still, that a house is often not the best way to honor the life and work of a writer. Writers' house museums rarely increase tourism, despite the hopes of their founders. They are expensive to maintain. They get foreclosed on, and the heaters break down. And they will never get it right: they will never fuse author, text, and reader together in a tight economy. So save your money and pass on the Shteyngart apartment.

But I no longer scoff at those who do want to build them, from the Fairfax Renaissance group to the women who preserved Orchard House over a century ago. We pick and choose our stories. The ones we want to hear offer us something we need to hear, be it solace, support or a cautionary tale. The stories that resonate change as do we, individually and collectively. I did, over the years of my travels. And so did America since we started building these odd little memorials. The fear of promoting Louisa May Alcott as a suffragist seems politically problematic to us now, but it was an important one then. That story is preserved in Alcott's house, though it is harder to find than the Jo dolls in the gift shop. Someday, perhaps, my reverence for the caretakers of the Dunbar house may seem sentimental or rearguard. In a generation Jack London may get his wish and be lauded as a pioneering sustainable farmer, and forgotten as an author. Who knows? The narratives the houses tell will circulate, whether or not they are "true," should they satisfy a need.

And though the houses do struggle to bring in tourists, if we add all the Americans who visited a writer's house last year, the total would be in the hundreds of thousands. That means a good number of Americans take time on their weekends or make trips on their vacations to pay an admission fee, maybe even dragging the kids, to walk through drafty, melancholy houses in which not much happens. Not one—not even in Key West—has a reenactor scribbling furiously at his desk to entertain the crowds.

I do not find what I am supposed to in these houses, because the displays and guides do not speak to me. But every so often I find a genuine touchstone, a piece of the literary cross: LaVerne Sci reciting Dunbar, the inmates signing at the jail across from Whitman's house, the forgotten history of Louisa May Alcott's vortices in her Boston garret, Tom Mahon in Asheville, Taylor Paslay in an empty living room in Ketchum, or the stones of Jack London.

Writers' house museums are fictions and we the visitors their readers. We get to make meaning out of them, not they from us. Maybe Barthes was right, after all. The houses, like books, are re-created in our imaginations, and once inside we can experience them any way we choose. We can be snarky, or reverent, or anachronistic, insist upon empirical verity, or decry their very existence, depending on our relationship to the author, to the place, to ourselves. I have done all of the above over the years. We can dance on top of the wide-planked pine flooring upon which someone now dead once walked, or send a Hallmark card, or yawn, or leave a rock, or plant a garden. We wear the bootsoles. We make our own impressions.

What was it that I was looking for all those years after all? Why did I go? I was seeking to find the place of literature in America today—not just way back when, when the author was alive, or when the houses were preserved, but also here and now. And I wanted to find a place for myself in it where I could live comfortably. Over the years I have moved from a big house to a smaller one, and my family has shrunk, too, but I am calmer in my new space. In the house of my imagination—or, as Emerson put it, in the house my spirit has built—I have gone the other direction, into a more expansive dwelling than when I stayed within the walls of academe. This place has an unruly blueprint, is prone to leaks, and is often a mess. It suits me.

American Writers' Houses Open to the Public

This list focuses on people who are primarily remembered for their literary work; therefore, I do not include houses like the Theodore Roosevelt house, though the President did write books as well. I only include houses open for tours; many other houses are preserved but not listed here, or open for vacation rentals but not tours. Given these and other vagaries, this list should not be considered definitive.

Louisa May Alcott

Orchard House, 399 Lexington Road, Concord, Massachusetts 01742. Tel: 508-369-4118. Run by the Louisa May Alcott Memorial Foundation. www.louisamayalcott.org.

Thomas Bailey Aldrich

Thomas Bailey Aldrich Memorial, P.O. Box 300, Portsmouth, New Hampshire 03802. Tel: 603-433-1100. Run by Strawbery Banke. www.strawberybanke.org.

Louis Bromfield

Malabar Farm, 4050 Bromfield Road, Lucas, Ohio 44843. Tel: 419-892-2784. Run by the Malabar Farm Foundation (located within Ohio State Parks/Department of Natural Resources). www.malabarfarm.org.

William Cullen Bryant

W. C. Bryant Homestead, Route 112, Cummington, Massachusetts 01026. Tel: 413-634-2244. Run by Trustees of Reservations [Massachusetts]. www.thetrustees.org/pages/285_bryant_homestead.cfm.

Cedarmere, Bryant Avenue, Roslyn Harbor, New York 11576. Tel: 516-571-8130. Run by the Bryant Library. www.nassaulibrary.org/bryant/Localhist/cedrmer.htm.

Pearl S. Buck

Pearl Buck House, 520 Dublin Road, Perkasie, Pennsylvania 18944. Tel: 215-249-0100. As of 2010: closed for renovations. Run by Pearl S. Buck International. www.psbi.org.

Pearl S. Buck Birthplace, U.S. Highway 219, P.O. Box 126, Hillsboro, West Virginia 24946. Tel: 304-653-4430. Run by the Pearl S. Buck Birthplace Foundation, Inc. www.pearlsbuckbirthplace.com.

Thornton W. Burgess

Thornton W. Burgess Museum, 4 Water Street (Route 130), Sandwich, Massachusetts 02563. Tel: 508-888-4668. Run by the Thornton W. Burgess Society. www.thorntonburgess.org.

John Burroughs

Slabsides, Floyd Ackert Road and Burroughs Drive, West Park, New York 12493. Tel: 845-384-6320. Run by the John Burroughs Association. http://research.amnh.org/burroughs/slabsides.html.

Willa Cather

Willa Cather Childhood Home, 413 North Webster Street, Red Cloud, Nebraska 68970. Tel: 402-746-2653. Run by the Willa Cather Pioneer Memorial and Educational Foundation. www.willacather.org.

Emily Dickinson

Emily Dickinson Homestead, 280 Main Street, Amherst, Massachusetts 01002. Tel: 413-542-8161. Run by Amherst College. www.emilydickinsonmuseum.org.

Frederick Douglass

Cedar Hill, Frederick Douglass National Historic Site. Visitor Center, 1411 W Street SE, Washington, D.C. 20020. Tel: 1-877-444-6777. Run by the National Park Service. http://www.nps.gov/frdo/planyourvisit/guidedtours.htm.

Paul Laurence Dunbar

Paul Laurence Dunbar House, 219 Paul Laurence Dunbar Street, Dayton, Ohio 45407. Tel: 937-224-7061. Run by the Ohio Historical Society. www.ohiohistory.org/places/dunbar/.

Ralph Waldo Emerson

Ralph Waldo Emerson House. Tel: 978-369-2236.

William Faulkner

Rowan Oak, Old Taylor Road, Oxford, Mississippi 38655. Tel: 662-234-3284. Run by the University of Mississippi.

F. Scott Fitzgerald

F. Scott and Zelda Fitzgerald Museum. 919 Felder Avenue, Montgomery, Alabama 36106. Tel: 334-264-4222. Run by Fitzgerald Museum. http://www.fitzgeraldmuseum .net/about_us.html

Robert Frost

Robert Frost Farm, State Route 28, Derry, New Hampshire 03038. Tel: 603-432- 3091. Run by New Hampshire Division of Parks and Recreation. www.nhstateparks .org/ParksPages/FrostFarm/Frost.html.

The Frost Place, off Route 116, Franconia, New Hampshire 03580 Tel: 603-823- 5510. Run by the City of Franconia.

Hamlin Garland

Hamlin Garland Homestead, 357 West Garland Street, West Salem, Wisconsin 54669. Tel: 608-786-1399. Run by the West Salem Historical Society.

Zane Grey

Zane Grey Museum, Scenic Drive, Lackawaxen, Pennsylvania 18435. Tel: 570-685- 4871. Run by the National Park Service. www.nps.gov/upde/zgmuseum.htm.

Jupiter Hammon

Lloyd Manor, Lloyd Lane and Lloyd Harbor Roads, Lloyd Harbor, New York 11743. Tel: 631-692-4464. Run by the Society for the Preservation of Long Island Antiquities. www.splia.org/museum_lloyd.html.

Joel Chandler Harris

The Wren's Nest, 1050 Ralph David Abernathy Boulevard, Atlanta, Georgia 30310. Tel: 404-753-7735. www.wrensnestonline.com.

Nathaniel Hawthorne

Nathaniel Hawthorne Birthplace, 54 Turner Street, Salem, Massachusetts 01970. Tel: 978-744-0991. Run by the House of the Seven Gables. www.7gables.org.

The Old Manse, 269 Monument Street, Concord, Massachusetts 01742. Tel: 978- 369-3909. Run by the Trustees of Reservations. http://www.thetrustees.org/ places-to-visit/greater-boston/old-manse.

The Wayside, 455 Lexington Road, Concord, Massachusetts. Tel: 978-318-7826. Run by National Park Service. http://www.nps.gov/archive/mima/wayside/index1.htm (also home of Louisa May Alcott and Margaret Sidney).

Ernest Hemingway

Hemingway Birthplace House, 339 N. Oak Park Avenue, Oak Park, Illinois 60302. Tel: 708-848-2222. Run by the Hemingway Foundation of Oak Park. www.ehfop.org.

Ernest Hemingway Home and Museum, 907 Whitehead Street, Key West, Florida 33040. Tel: 305-294-1136. Run by the Hemingway Home and Museum. www.heming wayhome.com.

O. Henry [William Sydney Porter]

O. Henry Museum, 409 East Fifth Street, Austin, Texas 78701. Tel: 512-472-1903. Run by Austin Parks and Recreation Department http://www.ci.austin.tx.us/ohenry/default.htm.

O. Henry House, 600 Lone Star Boulevard, San Antonio, Texas 78204. Tel: 512-226-8301.

Washington Irving

Sunnyside, West Sunnyside Lane, Tarrytown, New York 10591. Tel: 914-591-8763. www.hudsonvalley.org/web/sunn-main.html.

Robinson Jeffers

Tor House, 26304 Ocean View Avenue, Carmel, California 93923. Tel: 831-624-1813. Run by Robinson Jeffers Tor House Foundation. www.torhouse.org.

Sarah Orne Jewett

Sarah Orne Jewett House, 5 Portland Street, South Berwick, Maine 03908. Tel: 207-384-2454. Run by Historic New England. www.spnea.org/visit/homes/jewett.htm.

Helen Keller

Ivy Green-Helen Keller Birthplace, 300 West North Commons, Tuscumbia, Alabama 35674. Tel: 256-383-4066. Run by the Helen Keller Birthplace Foundation, Inc. www.helenkellerbirthplace.org.

Frances Parkinson Keyes

Beauregard-Keyes House, 1113 Chartres Street, New Orleans, Louisiana 70116. Tel: 504-523-7257. www.bkhouse.org.

Sidney Lanier

Sidney Lanier Birthplace, 935 High Street, Macon, Georgia 31201. Tel: 478-743-3851. Run by the Middle Georgia Historical Society. www.cityofmacon.net/Living/slcottage.htm.

Sinclair Lewis

Sinclair Lewis Boyhood Home, 810 Sinclair Lewis Avenue, Sauk Centre, Minnesota 56378. Tel: 320-352-5201. www.exploreminnesota.com/listing/index.cfm?id = 8496.

Vachel Lindsay

Vachel Lindsay Home. 603 South Fifth Street, Springfield, Illinois 62703. Tel: 217-524-0901. Run by the Illinois Historic Preservation Agency. www.illinoishistory.gov/hs/vachel_lindsay.htm

Jack London

Jack London State Historic Park, 2400 London Ranch Road, Glen Ellen, California 95442. Tel: 707-938-5216. Run by Sonoma County Regional Parks. http://parks.sonoma.net/JLPark.html.

Henry Wadsworth Longfellow

Longfellow National Historic Site, 105 Brattle Street, Cambridge, Massachusetts 02138. Tel: 617-876-4491. Run by the National Park Service. www.nps.gov/long.

Wadsworth-Longfellow House, 489 Congress Street, Portland, Maine 04101. Tel: 207-774-1822. Run by the Maine Historical Society. www.mainehistory.org.

Herman Melville

Arrowhead, 780 Holmes Road, Pittsfield, Massachusetts 01201. Tel: 413-442-1793. Run by the Berkshire Historical Society. www.mobydick.org.

Melville Home, 2 114th Street, Troy, New York 12182. Tel: 518-235-3501. Run by the Lansingburgh Historical Society.

Margaret Mitchell

Mitchell House and Museum, 990 Peachtree Street, Atlanta, Georgia 30309. Tel: 404-249-7015. Run by the Margaret Mitchell House and Museum. www.gwtw.org.

Christopher Morley

Knothole, Searington Road, Roslyn-North Hills, New York 11576. Tel: 516-571-8113. Run by Nassau County Parks. www.nassaucountyny.gov/agencies/Parks/WheretoGo/active/morley.html.

John Muir

John Muir National Historic Site, 4202 Alhambra Avenue, Martinez, California 94553. Tel: 925-228-8860. Run by the National Park Service. www.nps.gov/jomu.

Flannery O'Connor

Flannery O'Connor Childhood Home, 207 East Charlton Street, Savannah, Georgia 31401. Tel: 912-233-6014. Run by the Flannery O'Connor Home Foundation. www.flanneryoconnorhome.org.

Andalusia Farm, Milledgeville, Georgia 31059. Tel: 478-454-4029. Run by the Andalusia Foundation, Inc. www.andalusiafarm.org.

Eugene O'Neill

Tao House, Eugene O'Neill National Historic Site, P.O. Box 280, Danville, California 94526. Tel: 925-838-0249. Reservations required. Run by the National Park Service. www.nps.gov/euon.

John Howard Payne

Home Sweet Home Museum, 14 James Lane, East Hampton, New York 11937. Tel: 631-324-0713.

Edgar Allan Poe

Edgar Allan Poe National Historic Site, 532 N. Seventh Street, Philadelphia, Pennsylvania 19123. Tel: 215-597-8780. Run by the National Park Service. www.nps.gov/edal.

Edgar Allan Poe Cottage, Grand Concourse and East Kingsbridge Roads, Bronx, New York 10467. Tel: 718-881-8900. Run by the Bronx County Historical Society. www.bronxhistoricalsociety.org/poecottage.html.

Baltimore Poe House and Museum, 203 North Amity Street, Baltimore, Maryland 21222. Tel: 410-396-7932. Run by the Baltimore Commission for Historical and Architectural Preservation. www.eapoe.org/balt/poehse.htm.

William Hickling Prescott

William Hickling Prescott House, 55 Beacon Street, Boston, Massachusetts 02108. Tel: 617-742-3190. Run by the National Society of the Colonial Dames of America. www.nscda.org/ma.

Marjorie Kinnan Rawlings

Marjorie Kinnan Rawlings Historic Site, 18700 S. CR 325, Cross Creek, Florida 32640. Tel: 352-466-3672. Run by Florida State Parks. www.floridastateparks.org/marjoriekinnanrawlings.

James Whitcomb Riley

James Whitcomb Riley Birthplace and Museum, 250 West Main Street, Greenfield, Indiana 46140. Tel: 317-462-8539.

James Whitcomb Riley Home, 528 Lockerbie Street, Indianapolis, Indiana 46202. Tel: 317-634-4474. Run by the Riley Children's Foundation. www.rileykids.org/museum/.

Theodore Roethke

Theodore Roethke House, 1805 Gratiot, Saginaw, Michigan 48602. Tel: 989-280-6499. Run by the Friends of Theodore Roethke. www.roethkehouse.org/.

Carl Sandburg

Carl Sandburg Birthplace, 331 East 3rd Street, Galesburg, Illinois 61401. Tel: 309-342-2361. Run by the Illinois Historic Preservation Agency. www.state.il.us/HPA/hs/Sandburg.htm.

Carl Sandburg Home National Historic Site, 1928 Little River Road, Flat Rock, North Carolina 28731. Tel: 828-693-4178. Run by the National Park Service. www.nps.gov/carl.

Anne Bethel Spencer

Spencer House and Garden, 1313 Pierce Street, Lynchburg, Virginia 24501. Tel: 434-845-1313. Run by the Anne Spencer Memorial Foundation. www.annespencermuseum.com.

Edna St. Vincent Millay

Steepletop, East Hill Road, northeast of Austerlitz, Massachusetts. Tel: 617-547-5970. By appointment only. Run by the Edna St. Vincent Millay Society. www.millaysociety.org.

Harriet Beecher Stowe

Harriet Beecher Stowe House, 77 Forest Street, Hartford, Connecticut 06105. Tel: 860-522-9258. Run by the Harriet Beecher Stowe Center. www.harrietbeecherstowecenter.org.

Gene Stratton-Porter

Cabin in Wildflower Woods, five miles west of Kendallville, Indiana, on U.S. Highway 6 and three miles north on state route 9. Mailing: Box 639, Rome City, Indiana 46784. Run by the Indiana State Museum and Historic Sites. www.state.in.us/ism/HistoricSites/GeneStrattonPorter/Historic.asp.

James Thurber

Thurber House, 77 Jefferson Avenue, Columbus, Ohio 43215. Run by the Thurber House. www.thurberhouse.org.

Mark Twain

Mark Twain Boyhood Home and Museum, 120 North Main, Hannibal, Missouri 63401. Tel: 573-221-9010. Run by Mark Twain Home Foundation. www.marktwainmuseum.org.

Mark Twain House, 351 Farmington Avenue, Hartford, Connecticut 06105. Tel: 860-247-0998. Run by the Mark Twain House and Museum. www.marktwainhouse.org.

Noah Webster

Noah Webster House, 227 South Main Street, West Hartford, Connecticut 06107. Tel: 860-521-5362. Run by the Museum of West Hartford History. www.noahwebster house.org.

Edith Wharton

The Mount, 2 Plunkett Street, Box 974, Lenox, Massachusetts 01240. Tel: 413-637-1899. Run by The Mount. www.edithwharton.org.

Walt Whitman

Walt Whitman House, 328 Mickle Boulevard, Camden, New Jersey 08103. Tel: 856-964-5383. Run by the New Jersey Division of Parks and Forestry. www.nj.gov/ dep/parksandforests/historic/whitman/.

Whitman Birthplace, 246 Old Walt Whitman Road, West Hills, New York 11746. Tel: 631-427-5240. Run by the Walt Whitman Birthplace Association. www.charity advantage.com/waltwhitman.

John Greenleaf Whittier

Whittier Home, 86 Friend Street, Amesbury, Massachusetts 01913. Tel: 978-388-1337. Run by the Whittier Home Association.

Laura Ingalls Wilder

Laura Ingalls Wilder Historic Homes, 105 Olivet Avenue, De Smet, South Dakota 57231. Tel: 800-880-3383. Run by the L. I. Wilder Memorial Society, Inc. www.liwms .com.

Thomas Wolfe

Wolfe Memorial, 52 North Market Street, Asheville, North Carolina 28801. Tel: 828-253-8304. Run by the North Carolina Department of Cultural Resources. www .wolfememorial.com.

Notes

Chapter 1. The Irrational Allure of Writers' Houses

1 **"How quiet, serene . . . was written here":** Lockhart Steele, "On the Market: Gary Shteyngart Selling in LES," *Curbed*, April 14, 2009. http://curbed.com/archives/2009/04/14/onthemarketauthorgaryshteyngartsellingonles.php.

2 **two bloggers from DowntownNY:** "Let's Go See the 'Mystery Writer' Apartment!" *DowntownNY*, April 21, 2009. http://www.downtownyblog.com/2009/04/lets-go-see-mystery-writer-apartment.html

2 *New York Times:* Elizabeth A. Harris, "How to Spot a Good Deal." *New York Times*, 19 June 2009.

2 **"It needs a bit of work, and most buyers don't want a project":** Jhoanna Robledo, "Intelligencer," *New York* October 14, 2007.

2 *Guardian:* "Writers' Room: Margaret Drabble," *Guardian* July 6, 2007.

2 *O at Home:* "Legendary Writers' Homes," *O at Home: The Oprah Magazine* 2008.

2 **Coffee-table books:** J. D. McClatchy, *American Writers at Home* (New York: Library of America, 2004); Francesca Premoli-Drovlens, *Writers' Houses* (New York: Vendome, 2002).

3 **Petrarch's birthplace:** Harald Hendrix, "The Early Modern Invention of Literary Tourism: Petrarch's Houses in France and Italy," in *Writers' Houses and the Making of Memory*, ed. Harald Hendrix. (New York: Routledge, 2007), 15–30.

3 **Shakespeare's house:** Nicola Watson, *The Literary Tourist: Readings and Places in Romantic and Victorian Britain* (London: Palgrave Macmillan, 2008), 12.

3 **Abbotsford:** Watson, *The Literary Tourist*, 93–106.

3 **Henry Wadsworth Longfellow house:** For this research I am enormously indebted to Hilary Iris Lowe.

4 **Alfred Lord Tennyson's Farringford house:** Maev Kennedy, "New Tennyson Museum Marks the Bicentenary of the Poet's Birth," *Guardian*, August 6, 2009.

4   **fifty-six museums:** See list at the back of the book. This number is an approximation and excludes houses that do not allow tours, houses of public figures better known for other endeavors but who also wrote, such as Theodore Roosevelt, houses that were open but have now closed, and writers' houses that I have not discovered.

4   **Langston Hughes's old home:** Sandra Livingston, "Cleveland Nonprofit Aims to Revive Local House Where Writer Langston Hughes Lived as a Teen," *Cleveland Plain Dealer,* November 12, 2009.

4   **replica of Uncle Tom's Cabin:** Art Jester, "Replica of Uncle Tom's Cabin to Be Built in Kentucky," *USA Today,* December 5, 2009.

4   **Norman Mailer's house:** K. C. Myers, "Mailer Home Inspires Young Writers," *Cape Cod Times,* November 6, 2009.

8   **ceiling of Emily Dickinson's house:** Charles McGrath, "Ceiling Collapses at Dickinson House," *New York Times,* October 28, 2008.

8   **the Mark Twain house:** "Financial Woes May Force Closure of Mark Twain's Historic Home," *Poets and Writers,* June 4, 2008.

9   **Brock Clarke's 2007 novel:** Brock Clarke, *An Arsonist's Guide to Writers' Homes in New England* (Chapel Hill: Algonquin, 2007).

9   **T. S. Eliot house price:** email to author from David Chinitz, July 9, 2008.

9   **"The home . . . race habit":** Charlotte Perkins Gilman, *The Home: Its Work and Influence* (New York: AltaMira, 2002), 40–51.

11   **Thomas L. Masson, "Ten Houses for Ten Authors,"** *Country Life* (April 1924): 37–42.

12   **"usually with the hostess . . . other houses after all":** F. Scott. Fitzgerald, "An Author's House," *Esquire* (July 1936). There is a recent parody of this genre, the brilliant *Dictators' Homes* by Peter York, which takes shelter magazine profiles to their logical extremes. (To "Get The Look" York advises you should "Big It Up," "Go For Gold (Starting With Taps)" and "Have Yourself Everywhere.") Peter York, *Dictators' Homes: Lifestyles of the World's Most Colorful Despots* (London: Atlantic Books, 2005).

Chapter 2. Trying to Find Whitman in Camden

16   **"We know that . . . death of the Author":** Roland Barthes, "The Death of the Author," *Image Music Text* (New York: Hill and Wang, 1977), 148.

17   **"They just try . . . 'I love you'":** "Closing a Window to the World: Camden County Inmates Are About to Lose Their Link to the Outside," *Philadelphia Inquirer,* November 8, 1992.

17   **Whitman wrote prolifically:** Justin Kaplan, *Walt Whitman: A Life* (New York: Simon and Schuster, 1986).

18   **"Camden . . . brought me blessed returns":** James E. Miller, Jr., *Walt Whitman* (New York: Twayne, 1962), 50.

19   **"In these Leaves everything is literally photographed"**: Walt Whitman, *Leaves of Grass* (New York: Library of America, 1966), 39.

19   **"The United States themselves are essentially the greatest poem"**: Preface to *Leaves of Grass*, 449.

19   **"Rather than having . . . no appeal"**: Horace Traubel, *With Walt Whitman in Camden* (New York: Harvard College Library, 1908), 3: 553.

19   **"no parent . . . a solemn silence"**: Plato, *Phaedrus*, ed. Benjamin Jowett. (New York: Echo Library, 2004), 67.

21   **"Camerado! . . . triumphant, dead"**: Whitman, "So Long," *Leaves of Grass*, 609.

21   **"known to the world . . . dying here"**: "Closing a Window to the World."

21   **everyone on the streets of Camden**: Theodore F. Wolfe, *Literary Shrines: The Haunts of Some Famous American Authors* (Philadelphia: J. B. Lippincott, 1895), 201–217.

22   **"sandy monotonous waste . . . rented cheap"**: Elbert Hubbard, *Little Journeys to the Homes of Famous People* (New York: Putnam, 1896), 163–183.

23   **"It is always painful . . . Oh!"** Traubel, *With Walt Whitman in Camden*, 3: 553.

23   **Whitman's tombstone and brain**: Kaplan, *Walt Whitman*, 50, 51, 53.

23   **successful local campaign**: Geoffrey Sill, "Mickle Street House [Camden, New Jersey]," *Walt Whitman: An Encyclopedia*, ed. J. R. LeMaster and Donald D. Kummings (New York: Garland, 1998).

23   **"shame Camden into a realization of its unique opportunity to elevate itself"**: Sill, "Mickle Street House."

24   **Whitman's house became the property of the State of New Jersey**: Sill, "Mickle Street House."

24   **"a weed-filled vacant lot . . . cans of soup"**: Stephanie Kraft, *No Castles on Main Street* (New York: Penguin, 1979), 164.

24   **"We drove to Camden . . . we throw anything"**: Mark Doty, "Letter to Walt Whitman," in *Visiting Walt: Poems Inspired by the Life and Work of Walt Whitman,* ed. Sheila Coghill, Thom Tammaro, and Ed Folsom (Ames: University of Iowa Press, 2003), 39–48.

25   **"Unscrew the locks . . . at last to me"**: Walt Whitman, *Whitman, Poetry and Prose,* ed. Justin Kaplan (New York: Library of America, 1996), 210.

26   **"To think of time . . . we quite indifferent"**: Whitman, *Whitman, Poetry and Prose,* 197.

26   **"If you want me again . . . I stop somewhere waiting for you"**: Whitman, *Whitman, Poetry and Prose,* 112.

Chapter 3. Never the Twain Shall Meet

Note to epigraph: Mark Twain, *Pudd'nhead Wilson's New Calendar*, 1897.

28   **Argentine writer Jorge Luis Borges**: Shelley Fisher Fishkin, *Lighting out for the Territory: Reflections on Mark Twain and American Culture* (New York: Oxford University Press, 1996), 27.

29   **"I knew the man . . . not able to pay for it"**: Mark Twain, *Following the Equator, Part 4* (Champaign, Ill.: Project Gutenberg, 2004), http://www.gutenberg.org/files/5811/5811-h/5811-h.htm.

29   **"soft, sappy, melancholy"**: Andrew Hoffman, *Inventing Mark Twain: The Lives of Samuel Langhorne Clemens* (New York: Quill William Morrow, 1997), 22–33, quoted on 11.

31   **sincerity:** Lionel Trilling, *Sincerity and Authenticity* (Cambridge, Mass.: Harvard University Press, 1972).

35   *Adventures of Huckleberry Finn: Tom Sawyer's Comrade* (Berkeley: University of California Press, 2001), vii.

35   **"We find a piece . . . if necessary"**: *The Oxford Mark Twain*, ed. Shelley Fisher Fishkin (New York: Oxford University Press, 1996), 165.

37   **"lie just like . . . contempt for him"**: Lionel Trilling, "Huckleberry Finn," in *The Liberal Imagination: Essays on Literature and Society* (New York: New York Review Books, 2008), 106.

38   **"human slavery . . . poverty almost universal"**: *What Is a "Real" Civilization?* Twain, "On Foreign Critics," speech delivered in Boston, April 27, 1890, in *Mark Twain: Collected Tales, Sketches, Speeches, and Essays, 1851-1890* (New York: Library of America, 1992), 942. As quoted in Fishkin, *Lighting out for the Territory*, 23.

39   **two different characters named Injun Joe:** See Fishkin, *Lighting out for the Territory*, 44–48.

40   **"To us our house . . . we could not enter it unmoved"**: Letter to Joseph Twichell, reprinted in *Mark Twain: A Biography* (New York: Harper, 1912).

41   **"I had nothing to say. . . a painful subject anyway"**: Mark Twain, *The Autobiography of Mark Twain*, ed. Charles Neider (New York: Harper Collins, 1990), 99.

Chapter 4. The Concord Pilgrimage

Note to epigraphs: Ralph Waldo Emerson, "Circles," in *The Essential Writings of Ralph Waldo Emerson* (New York: Modern Library, 2000), 400; Theodore Wolfe, *Literary Shrines* (Philadelphia: Lippincott, 1895), 17.

44   **Dante house:** I did, however, discover nineteenth-century plaques on walls of buildings around Florence sporting quotes from Dante's works that were relevant to the building, thanks to *Literary Florence: Walking Tours in Tuscany's Capital* by Elisabetta Properzi Nelsen and Christopher Concolino, and spent a marvelous few hours on a treasure hunt of sorts for the plaques. I also read a wonderful story about Dante's bones, which were shipped away and at one point substituted for fake bones, more proof that literary relics and tourism are a surprisingly transhistorical phenomenon.

46   **"attracts more pilgrims . . . evangels"**: Wolfe, *Literary Shrines*, 18.

47   **"a microcosm 'by the study . . . comprehended'"; "he dwelt in the centre . . . Concord"**: Wolfe, *Literary Shrines*, 19.

47   **"must therefore . . . I'm going home"**: quoted in Wolfe, *Literary Shrines,* 45.

48   **"Behind a row . . . home-like"**: Wolfe, *Literary Shrines,* 46.

48   **"To these plain rooms . . . cherishes its treasures"**: Wolfe, *Literary Shrines,* 48–49, 51.

50   **you can only discuss its maintenance and financing**: E-mail from Marie A. Gordinier, managing director of the Ralph Waldo Emerson House, September 4, 2008.

52   **number of visitors**: Lawrence Buell, *The Environmental Imagination* (Cambridge, Mass.: Harvard University Press, 1995), 320.

52   **"All sites of pilgrimage . . . image of painting"**: Victor Turner and Matthew Turner, *Image and Pilgrimage in Christian Culture* (New York: Columbia University Press, 1995), 6.

52   **"in an atmosphere of holy calm"**: Buell, *The Environmental Imagination,* 319.

52   **Walden was transformed into a sacred place**: See W. Barksdale Maynard, *Walden Pond: A History* (Oxford University Press, 2004). Subsequent quotes from other visits to Walden from Maynard, 160–182.

53   **"I knew I must . . . rowboats for hire"**: E. B. White, *One Man's Meat,* new ed. (New York: Harper & Brothers, 1944), as quoted in Maynard, *Walden Pond,* 244.

54   **Walden Woods Project**: See Maynard, *Walden Pond,* 300–312.

54   **"The one thing . . . a new circle"**: Ralph Waldo Emerson, "Circles," in *The Essential Writings of Ralph Waldo Emerson* (New York: Modern Library, 2000).

55   **"Every few weeks . . . despondent"**: Louisa May Alcott, *Little Women, Little Men, Jo's Boys,* ed. Elaine Showalter (New York: Library of America, 2005), 88.

56   **"There lived a Sage at Appleslump"**: For biographical facts about the Alcotts and subsequent quotes from Louisa, see John Matteson, *Eden's Outcasts: The Story of Louisa May Alcott and Her Father* (New York: Norton, 2007).

57   **"Poor Jo! . . . the inevitable"**: Louisa May Alcott, *Little Women* (New York: Penguin Classics, 2007), 432.

58   **"liberty is a better husband . . . ill considered marriage"**: As quoted in Matteson, *Eden's Outcasts,* 330.

58   **"I don't enjoy . . . except my sisters"**: As quoted in Matteson, *Eden's Outcasts,* 332.

58   **"'An old maid . . .' not inviting"**: Alcott, *Little Women,* 440.

59   **"not to harass the authors . . . pap for the young"**: Matteson, *Eden's Outcasts,* 420.

59   **"confirmed . . . woman's activity"**: as quoted in Patricia West, *Domesticating History: The Political Origins of America's House Museums* (Washington, D.C.: Smithsonian Institution Press, 1999), 44.

61   **they did not believe in suffrage**: See Patricia West, "Inventing a House Undivided: Antebellum Cultural Politics and the Enshrinement of Mount Vernon"

and "Gender Politics and the Orchard House Museum," in *Domesticating History*, 1–92.

Chapter 5. Hemingway's Breadcrumb Trail

Note to epigraph: Ernest Hemingway, *Death in the Afternoon* (New York: Scribner, 1932), 100.

69   **"It is queer . . . literary history":** For Hemingway's biography, letters and comments to critics, see James R. Mellow, *Hemingway: A Life Without Consequences* (New York: Da Capo, 1993), 569.

75   **Pauline spent $20,000 on it:** http://www.hemingwayhome.com/HTML/house.htm.

75   **"The house sold to Bernice Dickson in 1961":** Dickson opened the house to the public in 1964. The house is still owned by the Dickson family.

78   **"What was he doing . . . famous writer":** Hunter S. Thompson, "What Lured Hemingway to Ketchum?" *Rolling Stone*, 1961.

79   **"Forget running . . . no turning back":** Hunter S. Thompson, "Final Days at Owl Farm," *Rolling Stone*, March 10, 2005.

81   **"Our doctor . . . please be seated there":** Mary Hemingway, *How It Was* (New York: Knopf, 1976), 507.

84   **"the only living museum . . . in residence":** Hilary Hemingway and Carlene Brennen, *Hemingway in Cuba* (New York: Rugged Land, 2003), 104.

86   **"deliberately salvaged . . . correspondence":** Mellow, *Hemingway*, 562, 606.

86   **"everywhere . . . sense of one-upmanship":** Valerie Hemingway, "Hemingway's Cuba," *Smithsonian* 8 (August 1, 2007).

Chapter 6. Not That Tom Wolfe

91   **"I wrote ten thousand words today!":** This and subsequent quotes taken from David Donald, *Look Homeward: A Life of Thomas Wolfe* (Cambridge, Mass.: Harvard University Press, 1987), 173–176.

92   **"walked back and forth . . . arrested":** Carol Ingalls Johnston, *Of Time and the Artist: Thomas Wolfe, His Novels, and the Critics* (Columbia, S.C.: Camden House, 1996), 39.

92   **first Asheville reviews:** Ted Mitchell, *Thomas Wolfe: An Illustrated Biography* (New York: Pegasus Books, 2006).

93   **"the same people . . . the South (hah!)":** Quoted in Donald, *Look Homeward*, 218.

93   **"as a great 'exuberant' . . . 'Here's my book!'"** Quoted in Donald, *Look Homeward*, 229.

94   **"Wolfe . . . living past":** William Styron, "The Shade of Thomas Wolfe," *Harpers* 236 (April 1968), 100.

96   **"I enjoyed *Look Homeward, Angel* . . . I outgrew him, perhaps":** Kurt Vonnegut, *Letter to* Thomas Wolfe Review, Fall 1979. Reprinted in Mitchell, *Thomas Wolfe*, 324.

96   "pilfered recklessly . . . English instructor's accumulation": Alfred Kazin, *On Native Grounds* (New York: Harcourt Brace, 1942), 480.

96   "sometimes grand . . . more often tedious and tinged with hysteria": Robert Penn Warren, "A Note on the Hamlet of Thomas Wolfe," *American Review* 5 (May 1935), 191–208. Review of *Of Time and the River*.

96   "which has always been shaky . . . Faulkner, Hemingway and Fitzgerald": William Styron, *Architectural Digest* 1984. Reprinted in *Historic Houses: Thomas Wolfe Remembered* (Asheville: Thomas Wolfe Memorial, 1988).

98   "And all of it . . . '. . . and here is Time'": Thomas Wolfe, "Return" (Asheville: Thomas Wolfe Memorial, 1976).

99   "Each of us . . . yesterday in Texas": Thomas Wolfe, *Look Homeward, Angel* (New York: Scribner, 2004), 3.

102   "There's no immortality . . . Maybe not": Henry Louis Gates, Jr., *Loose Canons: Notes on the Culture Wars* (New York: Oxford, 1992), 11-12.

Chapter 7. Best-Laid Plans at Jack London State Historic Park

Note to epigraph: Robert Burns, "To a Mouse," *The New Penguin Book of Romantic Poetry*. ed. Jonathan and Jessica Wordsworth (New York: Penguin, 2001), 254.

104   "perfectly useless . . . act of concentration": Alan Shapiro, "Why Write?" in *The Best American Essays 2006*, ed. Robert Atwan (New York: Mariner, 2006), 205.

104   "I think that art . . . midst of distraction": Alfred Kazin and George Plimpton, eds., *The Paris Review Interviews Volume 3* (New York: Viking. 1967), 103.

104   "It is self-forgetful . . . space and time, dissolve": Shapiro, "Why Write?" 205.

105   "Come to see . . . and draft-horses": *The Letters of Jack London: Volume Three: 1913–1916*. ed. Earle Labor, Robert C. Leitz III, and I. Milo Shepard (Stanford: Stanford University Press, 1988), 1122.

106   "Do you realize . . . hand in hand": The biographical facts of London's life are from Alex Kershaw, *Jack London: A Life* (New York: St. Martin's Griffin, 1997).

106   "I believe the soil . . . the tourist groves": Charmian London, *The Book of Jack London*, volume 2 (New York: Century, 1921), 278.

106   "old-fashioned methods . . . putting nothing back"; "In the solution . . . basis of economics": C. London, *The Book of Jack London*, 273, 266.

106   "I adopted the policy of taking nothing off the ranch": C. London, *The Book of Jack London*, 273.

106   "so that instead . . . rich crops a year": C. London, *The Book of Jack London*, 277.

106   London's techniques: For a discussion of the influence of London's farming techniques today, see Adrian Praetzellis and Mary Praetzellis, "'Utility and Beauty Should Be One': The Landscape of Jack London's Ranch of Good Intentions," *Historical Archeology* 23 (1989), 33–44.

107   **"Have any of you . . . hills of California":** Clarice Stasz, *Jack London's Women* (Amherst: University of Massachusetts Press, 2001), 212–213.

107   **"What makes biography . . . empty French roads":** Hermione Lee, *Virginia Woolf's Nose: Essays on Biography* (Princeton: Princeton University Press, 2005), 1.

108   **"smoothes the folds . . . swarm of possibilities"** James quoted in Lee, *Virginia Woolf's Nose,* 1.

110   **"Everyone agreed . . . cement partitions":** C. London, *The Book of Jack London,* 261.

110   **The house:** A schematic drawing of Wolf House is reproduced in *Jack London Ranch Album* (Stockton Calif.: Heritage Publishing Company, 1995), 19.

110   **"It isn't the money . . . so much beauty":** C. London, *The Book of Jack London,* 262.

Chapter 8. The Compensation of Paul Laurence Dunbar

Note to epigraph: Ralph Waldo Emerson, "Representative Men," in *Seven Lectures* (Boston: Houghton Mifflin Harcourt, 1883), 33.

115   **Dunbar's reputation:** The biographical facts of Dunbar's life are taken from *Sport of the Gods and Other Essential Writings,* ed. Shelley Fisher Fishkin and David Bradley (New York: Modern Library, 2005), as well as from Eleanor Alexander's *Lyrics of Sunshine And Shadow: The Tragic Courtship and Marriage of Paul Laurence Dunbar and Alice Ruth Moore: A History of Love and Violence Among the African-American Elite* (New York: New York University Press, 2001).

121   **"the only man . . . the spoken language":** William Dean Howells, Introduction to *Lyrics of Lowly Life* (Salem: Ayers Company, 1992). As quoted in Dunbar, *The Sport of The Gods and Other Essential Writings,* 14.

121   **"I didn't start . . . write anything but dialect":** James Weldon Johnson, *Along This Way* (New York: Viking Press, 1933; rprt. New York: Da Capo Press, 2000), 160.

Chapter 9. Poe Houses and Arrested Decay

128   **"I think we should . . . American Shakespeare":** "To Save Poe's Home," *New York Times.* September 23, 1895.

136   **"I have been building . . . shanties of chapters and essays":** As quoted in Hershel Parker, *Herman Melville: A Biography, 1819–1851,* volume 1 (Baltimore: Johns Hopkins University Press, 2005), 847.

136   **Melville's earnings:** Andrew Delbanco, *Melville: His World and Work* (New York: Knopf, 2005).

Chapter 10. At Home with Charles Chesnutt and Langston Hughes

138   **Chesnutt, the quintessential American self-made man:** For biographical details of Chesnutt's life, see William L. Andrews, *The Literary Career of Charles W. Chesnutt* (Baton Rouge: Louisiana State University Press, 1980).

138   **"The object of my writing . . . crusade against it":** Charles Chesnutt, *To Be an Author: The Letters of Charles W. Chesnutt, 1889–1905* (Princeton: Princeton University Press, 1997).

141   **"so early and so finally"; "The enthusiasm . . . negative poetry"; "Since Eliot . . . remains problematic":** Quoted in Timothy Goeglein, "Poetic Injustice: Need for a Memorial to T. S. Eliot in St. Louis," *National Review,* May 29, 1995.

142   **"The progress of an artist . . . remarkable or interesting":** T. S. Eliot, "Tradition and the Individual Talent," in *The Critical Tradition: Classic Texts and Contemporary Trends,* ed. David H. Richter, 3rd edition (Boston: Bedford/St. Martin's, 2006).

143   **Foreclosure and sale:** http://blog.cleveland.com/metro/2009/07/housewhere langstonhughesli.html.

143   **"The only thing . . . read myself to sleep":** Quoted in Arthur Rampersad, *The Life of Langston Hughes, Vol. 1, 1902–1941* (New York: Oxford University Press, 2002).

144   **attempt to establish a Langston Hughes museum in gentrified Harlem:** "Putting Poetry Back into Langston Hughes' House," *New York Times,* April 9, 1995, City Weekly, p. 6.

Acknowledgments

I USED TO guard my ideas closely. During the time I spent mulling over, drafting, and revising this book, I learned how to share. My teachers were those I ran into on my travels through book-writing. They come to ideas with a generous spirit, intellectual joie de vivre and humor, and I owe them great thanks. Jerry Singerman understood what this project was about when I could not yet articulate it, gave it a home, and stood tough when I faltered. Denise Grollmus and Nikhil Swaminathan improved drafts so expertly I was left humbled. James Rowell, Cody Wiedwandt, and Marten Frazier offered invaluable research assistance, thanks to grants from Oberlin College. The Furthermore Foundation provided a grant to support my travel and writing. Earlier versions of chapters were published in the *Believer*, the *Oxford American*, the *American Prospect*, and *Fine Books and Collections*. I thank Heidi Julavitis, Marc Smirnoff, Ann Friedman, and Scott Brown, respectively, for their interest and edits. Gabriel Brownstein, Lawrence Buell, Jennifer Horne, Erik Inglis, Andrew Keen, Hilary Iris Lowe, Kristin Ohlson, Pamela Snyder, Susan Stewart, Evelyn Tribble, and Wendy Wasman took time to comment on drafts. The Trubeks—Dave, Louise, Jessica, and Amy—have been there all along. I am grateful to my travel partners and hosts Jane Alexander, Kate Julian, Philip Stevens, Andrew Weiss, and Dany Truby. I owe a debt to all the curators who took the time to talk with me, especially Chris Morton. Finally, a big high five to Simon, who makes my house ridiculously fun to live in.